The Paris Trilogy

Colombe Schneck

SCRIBNER

LONDON NEW YORK SYDNEY TORONTO NEW DELHI

First published in the United States by Penguin Press,
an imprint of Penguin Random House LLC, 2024

First published in Great Britain by Simon & Schuster UK Ltd, 2024

Seventeen first published in French as Dix- ept ans, Grasset, 2015.
Friendship first published in French as Deux petites bourgeoises, Stock, 2021.
Swimming: A Love Story first published in French as La Tendresse du crawl, Grasset, 2019.

1 3 5 7 9 10 8 6 4 2

Simon & Schuster UK Ltd 1st Floor
222 Gray's Inn Road London
WC1X 8HB

Simon & Schuster: Celebrating 100 Years of Publishing in 2024

www.simonandschuster.co.uk
www.simonandschuster.com.au
www.simonandschuster.co.in

Simon & Schuster Australia, Sydney
Simon & Schuster India, New Delhi

A CIP catalogue record for this book is available from the British Library.

Hardback isbn: 978-1-3985-2939-7
eBook isbn: 978-1-3985-2940-3
eAudio isbn: 978-1-3985-3178-9

Printed and Bound in the UK using 100% Renewable
Electricity at CPI Group (UK) Ltd

MIX
Paper | Supporting
responsible forestry
FSC® C171272

CONTENTS

Preface vii

SEVENTEEN *1*

FRIENDSHIP *55*

SWIMMING:
A LOVE STORY *147*

Acknowledgements 223
Bibliography 225

Preface

My childhood was utopian. I was not a girl, I did not have a girl's body, I was just me, Colombe: irascible, determined, stubborn, violent, brutal, frank, clumsy, thieving, lying, mistreating my dolls and spinning stories about them, bad at school unless the subject intrigued me. I danced and envisioned myself a prima ballerina, I rode horses and saw myself a champion equestrian, I ran as fast as I could, I skied at top speed, I got dizzy and couldn't climb the rope in gym class. I read all day. I loved fairy tales, mean old Scarlett O'Hara, and comic book stories about the race car driver Michel Vaillant and Rahan the prehistoric man. I wore Liberty-print dresses and denim overalls. I wanted to know all about love, I was in love with my teacher, wanted to know about sex, but not too soon, wanted to marry and be a mother, but not right away, I wanted to be left alone for as long as it took to find my place, to become who I was. I was an ambitious young person, desiring the most prestigious degrees, the right to choose, to decide. Except my body, little by little, betrayed me. This hair, these breasts, enormous. My period. I decided it didn't have anything to do with me, I let the blood flow, let it stain my underwear, my clothes.

When I was seventeen years old, I found out I was pregnant. I couldn't believe it. I was furious: my body had let me down. This wasn't what I'd been taught, I hadn't been warned about this. I'd grown up in the 1970s and '80s, in Paris, part of the intellectual bourgeoisie, where there was no difference between boys and girls, and *pow!* I had a girl's body, a uterus. I was pregnant and angry. Society had lied to me. I had believed what I had been taught in school, that the pronoun *il* was neutral, that I, too, belonged to *il* when the masculine took precedence over the feminine, that we were all included in the indeterminate group of *il*. It wasn't true, it was a lie, I was a girl, I was *elle* and I was less than and I had to efface myself. That boy in his male body could have as much sex as he liked, with no risk of getting pregnant, none whatsoever. Whereas I – I had to be careful. My father said to me (although he had always given me the opposite impression, admiring my ambition, my bad temper, my wilfulness): 'You're a girl, you must be careful with your body, it is fragile.' I was a girl, then, and, at seventeen years old, I had just found out. I was ashamed of it; I hunched over, hid my too-large breasts, my too-generous curves. I was ashamed and I was fragile. I had an abortion, and it's taken me thirty-five years and Annie Ernaux's example to talk about it.

Because this body had diminished me with its fragility, *pregnant*, its lack of neutrality, *pregnant*, this bizarre physical response, *pregnant*, its inability to do what I wanted it to, *pregnant*, imposing a state of being that didn't interest me at all, *pregnant*, I decided to let it go, this incompetent, banal body, and to invest entirely in my mind.

But my spirit let me down too: I had, for reasons I didn't understand at the time, reduced my ambitions, humbled my desires, hidden them, giving them a form that wouldn't frighten anyone and wouldn't take up too much space. I knew I mustn't talk too much; I was afraid of betraying myself. I kept my head down, I followed the others, I accepted my place in the body that was given to me. I became a mother, and it became normal to sacrifice myself for others, I didn't have a choice. In this way I accepted that my body was female.

I had accepted my gender identity, according to which I was summoned to have children, to cook, and to clean the house. I had my children and took great pleasure in them, I liked being a mother, I had finally become lovely and sweet. That was fine with me. Everyone else seemed happy. I could sometimes be rude. I bore the criticism: maybe I wasn't so sweet and lovely after all. I couldn't quite fit the mould of this female body.

I still cherished a few vague hopes for myself. I had some things to say, I started writing books, I got divorced, I was alone, I had to earn more money, I had to bring up my children, I needed what remained of my old wilfulness to do it. I raised up my head, said what I had to say, and heard in response:

you are egotistical, you are arrogant, who do you think you are? It didn't work with men, I wasn't a good wife, a good girl-friend, but I discovered that I was a good friend, that I was very good at those more free and open relationships, in which the roles were undefined and ungendered.

Then at fifty years old, while taking swimming lessons, I finally realised that my body was not actually as incompetent as I'd thought. My physical gestures had been, until then, small, worried, tense. In swimming I learned to extend them, to build up my strength and use it in the right doses. My gestures improved, became more fluid. I saw male bodies swimming beside me, and I swam past them, I was delighted, my breasts got smaller, my uterus stopped working. My body, by showing me who I was, allowed me to become fully myself: not a woman, but a living being who likes to put on make-up wear dresses and high heels, cook, do nothing, be in love, spend time with friends, have conversations, particularly with people with whom I disagree.

I THOUGHT I WAS a woman, something sweet and charming, who bends in acceptances of any hardship. I can tell you writing these texts transformed me. I have strong shoulders, two fists to punch with, you shouldn't mess with me. I can be arrogant, I don't care; I'm important, so are these three novellas. *Seventeen*, *Friendship* and *Swimming: A Love Story* narrate my bodily apprenticeship: this is my living body, this is my living spirit, that of a unique person, perpetually in motion, called Colombe Schneck.

SEVENTEEN

For Annie Ernaux

Your notebooks from high school
hold all your dreams and secrets
all the words you never say ...

—YVES SIMON, 'Diabolo menthe'

I never told anyone what happened to me in the spring of 1984. Not my ex-husband and children, nor my closest friends. The shame, the embarrassment, the sadness—

I never told anyone how I accidentally became an adult.

Last year, in an interview with the daily newspaper *L'Humanité*, Annie Ernaux recalled that 'a solitude without limits surrounds women who get abortions'.

She experienced this solitude in 1964. She was twenty-three years old. At the time, abortion was a crime punishable by law. She describes looking through libraries for books in which the heroine wants to terminate a pregnancy. She was hoping to find companionship in literature; she found nothing. In novels, the heroine was pregnant, and then she wasn't anymore; the passage between these two states was an ellipsis. The card catalogue entry for 'Abortion' at the library only listed scientific or legal journals, addressing the subject as a matter for criminal justice.

She felt even more resolutely cast back into her solitude, reduced to her social condition. Illegal abortion, in all its physical and moral brutality, was at that time a matter of obscure local rumour.

Even if today abortion is protected by law in France, it still exists on the margins of literature.

When, in 2000, Annie Ernaux published *Happening (L'évé-*

nement), a narrative about a clandestine abortion before the Veil Law (which legalised abortion in France), the book didn't make much of an impact. It was an upsetting story. A journalist dealt the following blow to her: 'your book made me nauseous'.

Abortion isn't a subject worthy of literature.

It's a war you come through, somewhere between life and death, humiliation, disapproval and regret.

No, it isn't a worthy subject.

I listened to Annie Ernaux. What she said about silence, about embarrassment, about how 'women can take nothing for granted' yet they 'do not mobilise enough'.

At a time when, here in Europe, legislation on the voluntary termination of a pregnancy is constantly called into question, when we hear about abortion becoming 'banal', when some people even go so far as to invent something called a 'convenient abortion', I find that I have to tell the story of my own 'happening': what it meant, and continues to mean.

Neither banal, nor convenient.

I have no choice; I have to talk about what happened in the spring of 1984.

I'm seventeen years old and I have a lover. I'm not in love but I have a lover. I sing as I cross the Boulevard Saint-Michel, I'm seventeen years old and I have a lover, and I am very happy. I am not like my mother, I am not her loneliness. I am myself, a girl who's sleeping with a boy without being in love with him. I am seventeen years old and I have a lover. Not a boyfriend, not a sweetheart, not some adolescent crush, a lover, something grown women have.

I am an independent woman.

It is 1984. The Left is in power. The death penalty has been abolished, the Fête de la musique has been invented, and the compact disc, they promise, cannot be broken.* The prime minister is thirty-eight years old, AIDS is, to me, a disease at once threatening and far away, the feminist revolution has ended in triumph. On television, we watch and listen to *Apostrophes*, *Droit de réponse*, and Claude-Jean Philippe's film club.† We are all intelligent and modern.

As I write this today, that world, which I thought indestructible, has ceased to exist. Comfort, parents, support, optimism, faith in power and in the women and men who embody it – all of it, gone.

---

*Fête de la musique happens annually across France on 21 June, to celebrate the summer solstice and the longest day of the year, with music on nearly every street corner in the country, played by professional musicians and enthusiasts alike, for free. The first one was held in Paris in 1982. The title is a play on words: *fête de la musique*, literally 'music celebration', and *faites de la musique*, or the imperative 'make music'.

†*Apostrophes* was a prime-time literary talk show, hosted by Bernard Pivot; it ran from 1975 to 1990. Six million people tuned in every week to watch guests like Vladimir Nabokov, Marguerite Yourcenar, Susan Sontag or Marguerite Duras. *Droit de réponse* was a frequently polemical and irreverent debate show, hosted by Michel Polac, which ran from 1981 to 1987. Claude-Jean Philippe's film club was a television programme called *Ciné-club*, which ran on various stations between 1971 and 1994, and showed a range of classic world cinema. The films were shown in their original language, with French subtitles.

My lover is a boy in my class. His name is Vincent, he lives on the Right Bank. He's tall, with tortoiseshell glasses. He's cute and he has a scooter. I'm not in love with him but I like him a lot.

I was the one who chose him. During this time, I am in charge of these things. I decide, I designate. Everything is so easy. I don't have to ask my parents' permission to stay overnight at his house, or to spend the weekend there.

I'm not afraid, I've read so many erotic scenes in books, I'm hungry to experience the gestures and sensations that so fascinate me on paper. Will it all be as arousing, luminous and exciting as it is in books? I read and re-read *Emmanuelle*: 'If she resisted, it was only the better to taste, bit by bit, the delights of letting herself go [...] the man's hand did not move. Using only its weight, it applied pressure to her clitoris [...] Emmanuelle felt a strange exaltation go up her arms, down her bare stomach, in her throat. A previously-unknown feeling of grey took hold of her'. Could it be that good?

We don't have as much experience with other people's bodies, we aren't lounging in first class on a flight from Paris to

Bangkok, I'm not wearing nylon stockings or silk underpants, the hand on me isn't a stranger's but a classmate's. We are in a seventeen-year-old boy's narrow bed, in a room that still bears the traces of childhood — a map of the world, a Snoopy poster, a plaid throw. I want nothing more than that, and him.

I don't tell him that he is my first, I don't want him to feel he has to be careful, or for him to think I'm inexperienced, or a prude. He is just the first of many, I hope. I make up some story about having been with an older man, but he is the man from Emmanuelle's plane, an American who barely speaks French.

We quickly learn to touch like they do aboard the flight from Paris to Bangkok. All that's missing is the smell of the leather seats. We are always ready to begin again, we never get tired of doing it. His skin is soft, his skin is hard. It's very good.

I AM DELIGHTED. I have rid myself of my virginity, lived as if in a novel, I feel even more liberated. It is only the beginning. I am ready to make out with the entire world.

And the next day, the first morning, Vincent's mother makes breakfast for him and his new girlfriend.

We are in that part of the world where a girl and a boy can spend the night together, with their well-meaning, indulgent parents in the next room.

That spring, one Friday evening, I am sitting between my parents on the sofa in the living room. We are chatting, and suddenly I ask them:

—You don't happen to know any gynaecologists, do you, in your group of friends?

They are doctors, left-wing, they live on the Left Bank, they are open-minded, charming, cultured. This question strikes them as completely natural. They are delighted that their daughter is asking their opinion. They take this consultation very seriously: to whom can they entrust their daughter's body? Sitting on the large leather sofa, in the bright rotunda of a living room, spacious and warm, they think it over.

My mother has a thing for Tunisian gynaecologists. She herself goes to Dr Lucien Bouccara, Lulu for short, who is also a friend of hers. That's how it works, on the Left Bank in Paris in the 1980s.

My mother is persuaded that the best gynaecologists are Tunisian. And that's not all: most of them also have blue eyes. For her it's a sign of professional competence.

I do not agree. I do not want anything to do with Lulu, or

Dr Bouccara, the man who delivered me and who comes to dinner at our house.

—I don't want to take off my clothes in front of Lulu, what are you, crazy?

My father has a different idea. He thinks I should make an appointment with Dr L., who is also Tunisian, to make my mother happy. He knows him, he's serious and gentle, with an office on the Rue de l'Université.

That sounds fine. I make an appointment. I go alone. In any case, I won't have to pay anything. I grew up with an implicit understanding according to which doctors do not charge each other money. Many things are given to me without a price tag, it is only a question of asking, of serving myself.

At the first exam, I don't remember being afraid, or having been in pain. I am confident, absolutely certain that everything is fine, that everything always works out.

Dr L. is friendly, and attentive, and takes the time to talk with me. On a sheet of paper he makes a few drawings with a felt-tip pen, explains how easily I can get pregnant. For now, while we wait for the pill to become effective, my boyfriend and I have to be very careful. And above all, I mustn't forget to take the pill every day.

I feel like I'm in biology class; I'm slightly bored, and don't listen to everything. It's very simple: I want to go on the pill, I need a prescription. I leave feeling lighthearted. Everything is so easy.

I'm studying for my exams, I'm wearing an agnès b. T-shirt with light blue and cream stripes, I'm sleeping with a boy, I'm on the pill. I'm not worried.

In all of history has any seventeen-year-old girl ever had so much freedom?

I have been allowed to read forbidden books for as long as I could read. My parents always find out later.

I have very precise ideas about what I do and do not like.

I am against: Patrice de Plunkett's editorials in *Le Figaro*, girls who wear too much make-up and dye their hair.

I am for: no one imposing any rule on me, ever.

After the two volumes of *Emmanuelle*, I read, with the same eagerness, *Story of O* and *The Blue Bicycle*. Then I read the magazine *Fifteen*, which teaches girls how to kiss boys, and Henri Tincq's articles in *Le Monde* on what's going on in the world of religion.

I am completely carefree. The first week, I take the pill every evening. After that, I sometimes forget. It's less interesting, no longer a novelty or a major event, just an obligation. I have trouble with obligations.

I discover *In Search of Lost Time* and nothing else matters. Nothing, that is, except sex, of course. Vincent and I explore each other's bodies, our earlobes, the tips of our noses, our ankles, the very soft skin behind each other's knees. Slide up the length of the thigh, the fold of the buttocks, linger, implore.

June is approaching, soon it will be time to take the *baccalauréat*.

In my high school the success rate is 99 per cent. The exam is basically a formality. All year long, the teachers have encouraged students to dialogue with each other, kindling our imagination and creativity. May '68 wasn't that long ago. Hasn't the time come to get rid of this reactionary exam? And grades? And rankings? And term papers? Does any of it actually mean anything? The teaching staff try to boost our confidence. Our professors are all left-wing. They, too, wear clothing from agnès b. It's convenient; there's a boutique across the street from the school.

Our school is the École Alsacienne, an experimental secular school that's been around for a hundred years but is still very modern. The director is Georges Hacquard, pedagogue and Latin scholar, kindly and generous. He knows all our first names, our stories, our strengths and our weaknesses. Yes, we have the right to have weaknesses. I don't listen in class, I don't do my homework, it's no big deal. I don't have to rebel against anyone or anything, not school, not my parents. Nobody forces us to obey, or to submit to any rule except that of responsibility to the collective and respect for other people. We have to make our own way, exercise our liberty, persevere with our will, be curious. Our parents and teachers have fought for that. We are the children of a new era.

My father has devised a version of family life that suits him. He lives on the Quai de la Tournelle, on the ground floor of a seventeenth-century *hôtel particulier*. There he receives his friends and mistresses. He is for: life, free love. He is against: monogamy, boredom, habit. On the weekend, he comes to see his wife and children in the Rue du Val-de-Grâce. I tell him, accusingly: 'You want to have your cake, eat it, and kiss the woman who baked it.'

Secretly, I think he's got the right idea. I wish so much that my mother would come out of her room, stop shying away from life.

From time to time, my father lets me use his apartment. I like to be there, I settle in, I study for the *bac*, I read. I'm also allowed to see Vincent there.

I look at the newspapers that pile up on the living room table. One day, I see a special issue of the Dossiers et Documents section of *Le Monde*, on the economic crisis. Another time, an issue of *Libération* from the winter. The editor in chief, Serge July, has written an editorial with the title: *'Vive la crise*!' Long live the crisis! I am intrigued and worried. Crisis? What crisis?

But it's true. In the neighbourhood we begin to see what they're calling the '*nouveaux pauvres*', the newly poor. Near my school, a woman with brassy blonde hair and prominent roots asks me for money. Not so long ago, she went to the salon to get her hair coloured, or bought a box of dye at the supermarket. She thought she was making herself beautiful and blonde, she had time to take care of herself. That time is over.

I glimpse the cracks that could appear in my world too.

My father leaves me alone for the weekend. He's off to hike in Megève. My boyfriend has gone back to his parents' house. I make myself something to eat for dinner, taramosalata slathered on toasted bread, my favourite.

At my father's place we kids don't have a room of our own. I sleep on a bench covered in a white woollen rug and Moroccan throw pillows.

That night, I lie down and cry. I don't recognise these tears. I thought I was the luckiest girl in the world, sitting on the big leather couch between my parents, comfortable and warm. But I am hurling myself against something hard, something I don't understand.

These are new tears. I alone have provoked them.

I am crying because – I'm sure now – I'm pregnant. And I'm alone.

And just like that, I've been ejected from my everyday world. I have entered a different one, a restricted one, where it is no longer a question of homework to do, films to see, friends to hang out with or avoid, but of life and death, of my life, my future, my freedom, of what is happening in my body, which could be new life or nothing at all and for which I am responsible.

How much time did I spend scrutinising my underwear, hoping to see blood there? One month, two months? April, May? I can no longer count, or remember.

This is impossible, how can this be happening to me? I don't smoke, I don't drink, I don't stay out late. I like to read. I like to be in bed with Vincent. I think about it at school, how we spend entire weekends in that narrow bed, facing the Snoopy poster. I can only think of that, and of pleasure, so far removed from my mother's own life.

I don't think this is distress, exactly. Distress, torment, that's what they went through before I was born, a long time ago, during the war. All of that, I thought at the time, was behind us.

I admire my mother, who talks about how she worked right up until the moment I was born, and went back to work two weeks later. Her patients were dumbfounded when she told them. They hadn't even noticed she was pregnant.

My mother looks after children with disabilities. She teaches us to make no distinction between them, the ones she looks after, and us, her own children. She's right to be away so much. They need her more than we do.

My mother is a feminist, as was her own mother. They fought for the right to study, and to work. For me, the word feminist doesn't mean anything. I don't need to be one. What use could it serve? 'My body belongs to me'. 'A woman without a man is like a fish without a bicycle'. 'A child if I want, when I want'. All those slogans from the '70s seem out-of-date to me. We take all that stuff for granted. My mother's struggle belongs to a world that no longer exists.

I wait. I don't remember the date of my last period, it was such a long time ago. I'm afraid, I'm assailed by doubt. Fear takes up more and more space inside me. I'm pregnant, I'm certain of it. I decide to forget about it. It's not like me to be pregnant, not to choose, not to be free.

I watch and wait, I look for traces of blood. Nothing.

I am trapped in my body: a girl's, not a boy's.

But that wasn't how I was raised. Boys and girls are equal. I have as much freedom as my brother, my mother has as much freedom as my father. I believe it's a choice she makes, not to practise her freedom. I am wrong. She is not free: she is trapped in her past. I am not free to have sex. I am pregnant and I don't want to be.

I have to take the *bac* in a month. I am pregnant. I am afraid.

In the end, I resign myself to seeing Dr L. I have a problem. The girl with no problems has to admit she has a problem. This is not good. I would like to have no reason to complain, to be without cares. I have failed.

The doctor prescribes some tests, and the next day, he calls. He wants me to come in as soon as possible, he'll make room in his schedule.

He's very sorry. 'It's exactly what I hoped would not happen to you.' I'm sorry too. I'm pregnant, and I don't even know how far along I am. He asks questions, but I don't have anything to say in response. I don't have an explanation or an excuse. He seems annoyed, as if it were his failure too.

—You have to tell me clearly what you want to do.

That, I do know.

—I want an abortion.

With Vincent, I speak quickly, I come right to the point. I do not want the fear I feel inside me to spread to him, fear of what could happen, this child, his child. There is no child, he is not going to be a father. I am pregnant, it's my fault. I am telling him just to keep him informed, because we spend so much time together, because we have fun together, exploring the possibilities our bodies offer us, acts which have led to this. I do not tell him that I've cried, or that I cry, that now I'm only pretending to be there, with him, in our adolescent games, that I've become part of a different world in which decisions weigh more heavily.

I have no doubt. There is nothing to hesitate over. There will be no child. We are high school students, we are going to take our exams, enrol in university, turn eighteen, go away for the summer, and when we come back, build our adult lives.

He listens to me without saying anything. *What if we kept it?* I don't even let him ask the question.

To keep it would be to give up. I want to go to Sciences Po, to be a journalist for *Le Monde*, anchor the eight o'clock news, give my opinion on the radio, read forbidden books, get married and have kids as late as possible.

I only want one thing: to go on as we were before, when I didn't cry alone in my bed, when my only real torment was my mother's silence and sadness, her childhood in the war, alone in a convent, cold and abandoned. Until this moment I had only the benign sufferings of a teenager, dreaming of freedom and bursting with ambition.

Now, for the first time, I'm becoming aware that there is something heavy obstructing my vision, narrowing what I can see.

I tell my parents with the same off-handedness as when, a few months earlier, I had sat between them on the huge brown leather couch in the living room and asked them for help navigating the early stages of my sexual life. It already feels like a memory from another era. This time, the off-handedness is entirely feigned.

My parents do not judge me. They do not raise their voices or reproach me. It is not the kind of news they want to hear, they like it when I tell them about my academic achievements, my development as a young woman who is constructing herself in a way that will please them.

I can still see myself aged eight, sitting in a camel-coloured leather armchair designed by Marcel Breuer, facing my father's desk, a thick, plain plank of glass. I can precisely recall the astonished look on my father's face when I tell him I'm writing a biography of Napoleon. Of course, all I was doing was copying out a book about his childhood in Corsica.

And here I am at seventeen, pregnant, like so many other girls, like Annie Ernaux, the daughter of a shopkeeper in Yvetot in 1964, like Marie-Claire, the teenager at the Bobigny trial in 1972. I have been trapped by the fact that I am a girl. I am no longer the kind of girl who can escape the world by writing the biography of Napoleon, or reading the autobiography of Lauren Bacall five times in a row, the summer I turned eleven.

I am a normal teenage girl.

My father invites me to lunch with Vincent at the Closerie des Lilas. He eats there three times a week. It is ideally located on the way to school.

My father is the kind of man who receives, counsels, helps, seduces, gives, amuses.

He wears faded pink sweaters, rust-coloured pants, light khakis, collarless shirts made to order at Arnys, he smells good, like lavender eau de toilette. Pour un Homme, it's called, by Caron. He is bald, short, he has a moustache and round metal-framed glasses. My father is very generous and very beloved. He tells his children: 'Parents owe their children everything. Children owe their parents nothing.' At the Closerie des Lilas, he invites young colleagues to lunch, gives them advice and support. Other people's dreams, including mine, inspire him. For him I could do anything, be a dancer, a journalist, a member of cabinet, a horseback rider, a seductress, a reader.

I know the menu by heart. Creamed mushrooms, poached haddock à l'anglaise, chocolate marquise. I confess my latest ambition. Ever since I heard Nicole-Lise Bernheim on *Apos-*

trophes talking about her life on the road, I want to be a foreign correspondent for *Le Monde* in New York. He approves.*

He often says: 'We mustn't speak of things that make us angry.'

Today he doesn't have a choice in the matter. We're talking about abortion. He doesn't lecture us. He simply says that this is the kind of thing that makes life difficult, later. I don't really listen to him, I don't want to be told that it's serious. At that time in my life, problems evaporate as soon as they appear.

I want to believe that it is enough to paint over this first crack, so it will disappear.

I don't tell my friends, though I've known them since kindergarten.

There is something shameful about having been so stupid.

They would say I had behaved irresponsibly. They would be right. The most cutting critiques are often the most justified.

---

*Nicole-Lise Bernheim (1942–2003) was an actress, journalist, and writer.

In her November 1974 speech to the Assemblée nationale, Simone Veil said: 'In spite of contraception, accidents are possible.' I was taking the pill, but I hadn't taken it conscientiously, I hadn't always paid attention. Do I have the right to claim it was an accident?

I was so carefree. My woman's body was so new to me, I didn't yet know that it would impose its own rules, limit actions, movements, freedoms. It does not entirely belong to me, can easily be transferred to someone else. I felt betrayed by it. It took away my liberty.

I TAKE MY EXAMS PREGNANT. No one knows. I think even I forget about it.

I take the RER to the exam centre in Arcueil. On the platform at Port-Royal, I look at the other students. They are the same age as me, they are going to take the same test, they are tense, some laugh nervously, smoke, fidget. I don't.

But I am like them. A teenager who reads all the time, doesn't smoke, doesn't drink, goes to bed early, eats fruits and vegetables, makes pizza and chocolate cake for her friends, a teenager who doesn't see how she can rebel against her parents, who would have found it unfair to rebel, since she has not known war. I don't want my parents to worry about me, I don't want to give them the slightest concern nor to complain to them, I want always to be tidy, perfect, cheerful.

Today, I've failed.

My father goes with me and Vincent to the clinic, and drops us off outside the front door. Nobody says anything. Not either of us, or the nurses, the anaesthesiologist, or Dr L. No one reproaches me, or looks at me suspiciously.

Morality doesn't come into it.

I watch each of them attentively, I can detect nothing. The doctors, the nurses, the anaesthesiologist, the auxiliary nurses, everyone is neutral, attentive and indifferent to the nature of the procedure. What is happening to me is banal, a simple curettage, unremarkable. I am alone.

I have very few memories of that day. I know the clinic well; my father fills in there a few times a week. They ask if I am Dr Schneck's daughter. I say yes. I think they're putting me to sleep. I wake up in a room. No one has brought flowers or boxes of chocolate. There is nothing. I cannot be consoled. It is my own fault I am here, because I didn't pay attention.

Only my father and mother know where I am.

I felt nothing. And I still feel nothing. A little fatigue, a twinge in the belly. Nothing to worry about.

My mother didn't come to the clinic. The two of us will never speak of what happened that day – not before, and not after.

My sister and I still laugh about the way she tried to talk to us about menstruation. We were around ten years old. She pokes her head through the doorway into the kitchen and addresses us both, hurriedly.

—Girls? You, ah, know what menstruation is?

We burst out laughing.

—Of course, they taught us at school.

She is relieved, and closes the door. That is the extent of our sexual education.

Thirty years later, at a literary festival in Lyon, her brother, my uncle Pierre Pachet, will read a passage from *Sans Amour*, his most recent book, which is a series of portraits of women who have given up on love. He was talking about my mother, whose name he changed from Hélène to Irène.

He describes how during the winter of 1943, when Irène is eleven and a half, and hidden away in a convent, she finds a brown spot on her underwear. Blood has flowed between her legs, and she doesn't know what it is. 'I imagined the anxiety she must have experienced, the pain and the stupefaction it brought on – what was it? Faeces? No, it had to be blood (internal bleeding, an illness? Had she done something wrong? Was she guilty from birth?).'

She was afraid of so many things – death, blood, cold, not being able to bathe or keep clean. To whom could she admit these fears? Until her death she kept this story of total abandonment to herself; she only told one friend, who, much later, spoke of it to her brother.

And I understand her, this terrified eleven-and-a-half-year-old Jewish girl who thinks she's going to die alone, hidden in this convent, with this blood that comes from who-knows-where. Everything blends together confusingly, the absolute necessity of hiding her identity, the anguished fear that she'll never see her parents again, and now the discovery of her body.

'Something had been broken, in the world or in herself,' wrote my uncle.

That evening, in the clinic, my father is there. He helps me out of bed. We go back to the house. To my mother's.

Her daughter, a high school student, has just had an abortion. What does she say to me when I come home? Nothing that I can remember. She doesn't ask if everything went all right. It's not the kind of question you ask after an abortion. She doesn't ask me if I'm sad, or relieved, or tired, or if I cried. She doesn't ask these kinds of questions.

Like every night, I take a bath and I go to bed.

The next day, I have a fever and a stomach ache. I moan, I complain, I can't go to the end-of-the-year party the school has organised to celebrate exams being over.

To my friends, kids my own age, whom I love, to whom I confide everything, I say nothing. I don't dare — I won't say *confess*, because I didn't commit a sin to be confessed. Rather, I don't want them to know of my sorrow. They wouldn't understand, I think; they are too innocent.

I said nothing at the time, or later on. I never spoke of it to anyone. Sometimes, I find I am on the verge of saying the word, of sharing my *abortion* with a close friend. And then I don't, I back off. Why this silence? Why do women keep quiet?

I'm ashamed.

Is there perhaps something dirty about abortion? No one reproached me at the time, not my parents, not Vincent; he could have accused me of having been careless, of having forgotten to take the pill, and yet I feel there's a kind of stain on me, made of blood, and excrement, and the earth thrown on coffins at gravesides. So I keep quiet.

But yes, actually I did talk about it once. I'm thirty-two

years old and I'm talking about this stain to a woman who is fifteen years older than me.

Her name is Claire Parnet. She is the most intelligent, the most beautiful, the most spiritual woman I have ever met. I am a little in love with her. I tell her two secrets that I've never shared with anyone else. My father's father was cut up into pieces and thrown into a suitcase. And I had an abortion.

My father shouts at me. The last time he was angry with me, I was six years old. It was the first day of primary school. That evening, he showed me the letters A and B. I pretended not to understand, not to recognise them or to know how to put them together. I was testing him. How far could I push him? Would he still love me even if I were a stupid little girl?

He got angry and gave me the only slap of his life.

How many times in my childhood did he tell me how sorry he was, how could he do such a thing, slap me like that. But it only made me laugh.

My father loves me unconditionally.

Today, I know very well why he's yelling at me: I have to stop complaining.

It's not because I want to go to this party and it's unreasonable, it's because I am almost an adult and yet I have behaved as though my actions have no consequences. He gave me the name of a gynaecologist, I was prescribed the pill, I was allowed to sleep over at my boyfriend's house, I was given everything I wanted and still I complained? He would never say it, but I know that when he and my mother were my age, they had nothing, they didn't have the right to do anything, especially to have sex.

My father, in his gentle, generous, calm way, invites Vincent and me to have a drink with him on the terrace of the café Le Bonaparte, one late afternoon in June.

We mustn't speak of things that make us angry, he doesn't like that, he exercises restraint, he must have prepared what he wanted to say to us in advance. He wants to help us grow up to become responsible adults. He knows he won't be around for much longer, that he has heart problems, is fragile, he had a first warning when he was forty-two, he won't always be there to fix things, to protect me from what we might call my absent-mindedness, or my indifference. He says that we shouldn't be like him, that we have to look after ourselves, that an abortion is no sin but, as with all mishaps, it's something to try to avoid in our lives, something that won't do us any good.

I don't really believe him. I am convinced it had been easy for me, whereas it had been difficult, violent even, for Simone Veil, who fought for the law legalising abortion to be passed.

I know about the Veil Law, it's very recent, exactly ten years old. I remember the debates, the insults, the accusations. Simone Veil wants another St Bartholomew's massacre, has made a pact with barbarians, abortion is compared to the Holocaust, etc.*

I remember my parents' indignation hearing an MP insult Simone Veil at a hearing in the Assemblée nationale. I have since learned that his name was Albert Liogier and that he apologised the next day.

I remember that photo of Simone Veil with her face in her hands, and how the pundits were very moved to see this woman in tears.

Later, in an interview, she will explain that she was not crying, she was exhausted, it was three in the morning, she had been fighting for two days, she hadn't slept. It wasn't a picture of a fragile woman crying. It was an image of a combatant.

I am grateful to her for holding the line. I am uncomfortable, embarrassed, because I escaped the distress she described ten years earlier at the Assemblée. Veil wanted abortion to be an anomaly, a last resort in an impossible situation.

I was not in an impossible situation. If I had had a child with a boy I didn't love, my parents would have helped, his parents too.

In 2014, the concept of 'distress' was deleted from the law. A conservative MP called François Fillon objected, arguing that it would lead to abortion becoming something banal, casual.

And I thought, then, François Fillon: *this body of mine, and those of all the other women, they don't belong to you. What hap-*

---

*The St Bartholomew's Day massacre took place in 1572, in which anywhere from five thousand to thirty thousand Protestants were killed by Catholic mobs across France.

pens inside those bodies doesn't concern you. You have no moral right, no right whatsoever to judge.

Simone Veil said: 'Abortion is always an ordeal and will always be an ordeal.'

I believe her implicitly, but it's not true for me. I believe that now that it's over, I won't think of it again. Yes, I fit into that category denigrated during hours of debate over the law: the abortion of 'convenience'. An easy, banal abortion, forgotten as soon as it's over. My mother saying nothing to her seventeen-year-old daughter who's just had an abortion. What has just happened has, doubtless, no importance at all. In silence, I hide it away.

Forty years later, a woman confides in me. She had an illegal abortion when she was seventeen, in 1966. The year I was born.

Suddenly I am this woman, I am that child. And I feel a searing pain in my belly.

In 1984 I will turn eighteen and I do not yet know that thirty years later I will be like this woman.

I'm eighteen years old, I've just had an abortion, I don't even know how many weeks along I was. Did the doctor do a sonogram to find out? I'm sure he did, but I don't remember it.

Was I past ten weeks, when the psychological or physical risks are greater? Maybe. I don't know.

I was a minor; did I need my parents' consent? No, I'm sure I didn't. I was so accustomed to doing exactly what I wanted, I was free to read all night, to sleep over at my boyfriend's place. I never asked permission to do anything.

Was I informed, as the law requires, of the risks? I don't think so.

Was I given eight days to think it over, to come to a reasonable and mature decision? No, I had other things on my mind, I was focused on my exams.

Was I given a lecture on morality in the form of a medical consultation, a speech in which a doctor would emphasise that an abortion was not something to take lightly but a serious decision with consequences that needed to be weighed and should be avoided if at all possible?

That day in June, on the terrace of the Bonaparte, the light is golden and the air smells of jasmine. Vincent and I sit obediently across from my father. A man in his fifties who looks like the writer Erik Orsenna in a collarless shirt and an Indian silk scarf is quietly chatting with a pair of teenagers in jeans and matching T-shirts. From the neighbouring table it would be difficult to tell that our conversation is a serious one.

The man talks, but the girl isn't really listening, he says that it's no small thing, that they should not believe they will emerge unscathed.

The girl wants to think of something else. She pictures herself with another boy, with whom she is secretly in love, a friend's older brother. If this had happened with him, would she have kept it? She tells herself yes, but minutes later thinks no, better not have children right away, she has so much she wants to do, so much life to live, before that.

I still believe that I was lucky, so lucky. I was not born ten years earlier, my name isn't Marie-Claire, my mother doesn't work at the post office, I haven't been charged with illegally obtaining an abortion in the criminal court in Bobigny, I'm not looking at six months to two years in prison. Marie-Claire was also seventeen years old when she had an abortion, in 1971. She had been raped by a boy the same age as her, a boy from school, a delinquent. She didn't dare report him. She was poor. In 1971, having an abortion meant going to prison for the poor, and to England for the rich.

Thanks to some people from work, Marie-Claire's mother found a woman who knew what to do. Three times she tried to insert the probe in Marie-Claire's vagina, and three times she failed, leading the girl to haemorrhage seriously. The boy who had raped her was arrested for stealing a car. To gain his freedom he told the police about Marie-Claire's pregnancy and abortion. They arrested her, along with her mother, the woman who inserted the probe, and the women from work who put them in touch. All of them were charged.

Their lawyer, Gisèle Halimi, warned them: 'You will need to call on all your courage and determination.'

Marie-Claire was acquitted. The judge determined that she had been suffering from 'emotional, social, and familial pressure, which she was unable to fight'. Her mother was ordered to pay a fine of 500 francs.

The violence and injustice of this trial are what led to the adoption of the Veil Law, two years later.

I tell myself that I'm lucky and, for once, it's almost true.

That day at the Bonaparte, I feel as though I've forgotten the anxiety of the previous weeks. And yet I am the same girl who lay alone in her bed and cried at night because what was happening to her was not the life she wanted.

Vincent is quiet. From what I can recall, he was sweet and

attentive, and wanted to help me. But did I ever really ask him his opinion? No. He has no say in the matter, I am the one who made the decision. I think he doesn't know, really, what he's dealing with, that he can't possibly know, that all of this only concerns him indirectly. Of course he's equally responsible for the situation, he wasn't being careful about contraception either, but I don't hold it against him. We are two teenagers. We have other things on our minds. My father is wrong: none of this can be very serious.

Thirty years later, I meet Vincent again, the boy from the spring of 1984. Our school has organised a kind of reunion, the anniversary of our having passed the *bac*. He is there, along with my friends from childhood and adolescence.

He knew my mother and father when they were alive, and me when I was a heedless young girl, in another world. There is also an absent presence between us, who would be an adult today.

Today, Vincent is a man, with a family.

Does he still think about the spring of 1984, the winter of 1985, or how he could have become a father? Does he have any regrets? Any remorse? Does he feel embarrassed, or ashamed, or sad? Has he told the mother of his children?

I could ask him these questions but I don't seek him out. It seems that nothing binds us, not even this absence conceived thirty years ago.

I recover, I'm furious at having missed the party for the *bac*, I'm already thinking of other things. Vincent invites me to stay at his mother's in the Luberon.

This is the first time I've heard of the Luberon, my father is delighted, he tells me it's very chic.

At the Gare de Lyon we run, we're afraid to miss the train to Avignon. For the first time I have trouble keeping up with Vincent, I'm out of breath. Is this the beginning of being 'scathed' like my father said?

In the train, Vincent admits that, for him, this whole situation has had a positive side, that it's brought us closer together. I reply yes, sure. I'm lying. I don't agree. This is about my young female body.

When we get home from our trip, I break up with him. I'm still thinking about my friend's brother. I'll break up with him, too, one day.

I think the abortion is behind me, that that story is over. I have returned to my world.

A world in which I am free to desire, to act of my own free will, to make choices, even if I know now how easy it is to fall.

I have to pay attention to my body, to myself, to my surroundings, to the things that happen, to the accidents that may occur.

I learn that the world I belong to – educated, civilised – can throw me out at any moment, for the smallest reason. Bad news on an X-ray, a stupid little shadow on my father's heart, an unfortunate encounter. During those years, the serial killer Guy Georges lurks in the parking garages of Paris, he kills the cousin of a friend of mine. Death, which we never thought about much, is there, close at hand.

I'm still afraid, at the end of every month, that I won't get my period. The fear will stay with me for twelve years, until the moment when, finally, I experience a new feeling: I don't want to bleed, I'm ready to become a mother.

Is what happened really over, do these stories ever really end?

There will be other boys, my father's death, a wedding, my mother's death, two children, periods of loneliness, other men.

But during all that time I continue to think of him, of the child I didn't have, who doesn't have a name.

It's the winter after the *bac*, I have a lover, I am in love, my parents adore him, he goes to a very good university, he's the son of some friends of theirs, he's perfect. We leave on a skiing trip.

And suddenly, even though what happened is behind me, I'm thinking about it. I'm afraid of giving birth, of being in pain, of being torn in half, look, I can see the head! It's a boy, he cries a lot, I don't know what to do, I am clumsy and ill at ease.

Later on, I still think about it. The absence returns. He would be six months old, a year old. I still don't know what I am doing. I have left his father. I'm eighteen, I'm alone with this baby and I still live with my mother. Poor baby, whose mother doesn't know how to take care of him. She doesn't have the patience, can't devote herself to him entirely. She resents him for keeping her from travelling, from meeting new people, from reading day and night, from napping and sleeping late, for robbing her of her frivolity, for being so dependent on her, for crying the minute she moves away from him.

When these images come to me I throw myself into my life

at university. The images return. I chase them away, I think of other things. They always come back.

He will grow up far from me. I don't think of him often. And then from time to time he returns, full of silent reproach.

I don't listen to him. I don't want him to bother me, I don't have the time to deal with it.

I go to live in London and then in New York. I imagine getting in touch with him, but I don't, not a letter, not a phone call. What could I possibly tell him? That it's hard, that I'm alone, that every day is a struggle? I don't want to tell him that my life without him is a failure. That perhaps in the end, his presence wouldn't have prevented me from living – not at all.

My father is dead. I am no longer protected from anything, I'm no longer calling the shots. I return to Paris, I meet another boy, he says to me, I'm going to ask you a question and if you give me the right answer, you'll get a present. He has my father's whimsy and generosity. We marry. He wants a child. I don't tell him about you. I don't tell him how terrified I am of being pregnant, of giving birth, of being awake all night feeding a baby. I prefer to keep it to myself. I get pregnant so easily. Now I know.

It doesn't take long at all to get pregnant. I am triumphantly happy. The fear I carried with you has disappeared. I am ready.

But it returns. Without a warning, you knock at my door. I don't want to answer. I don't feel guilty, just a little sad.

We are growing up together. You seem to distance yourself from me. I won't introduce you to your little brother. A perfect baby, who hardly ever cries, laughs all the time, has blue eyes. My mother, your grandmother, calls him her little love, whereas for you, she's never had a nickname. She never mentioned you, not even once. For her, you never existed. You didn't even have a name. I never tried to think of one for you.

You'll tell me, rightly so, that it's too late. You've grown used to not having a name, after thirty years.

Your grandmother dies too. No one tells you. I imagine you are sad not to have known her, and sad for me. You are the only one who has detected my distress, my isolation, the only one who sees through me, the valiant smiling soldier that I am, trying to hide my cracks. And you, are you one more or one less dead person in my life? No, you're not another dead person. You are an absence.

I cling to your little brother and your little sister, who has just been born.

What I am about to tell you is cruel. Forgive me for being blunt: they are the most beautiful, the most charming children in the world.

For them, I will never be able to give enough, my love is unlimited and indestructible. For them, I get out of bed every three or four hours during the night, to cradle them, feed them, change their diapers, clean their adorable little bottoms. I dress them in much too expensive clothing. I admired them and still admire them, now that they're becoming teenagers. Your little brother knows Greek mythology by the age of six, and thousands of other things I know nothing about. As for your little sister, I hide her away, I'm afraid someone will steal her from me. I worry about them if they're even a second late out of the school gates.

For you I feel neither fear, nor worry, nor admiration. I saved it all for them. I no longer even feel what I felt for such a long time, I don't feel guilty for neglecting you. I think of you and I am only sad.

You had to make do with the crumbs I threw you, once a year, in winter. I don't even know what day you would have been born, only roughly that it would have been sometime in January or February 1985.

You sacrificed yourself for them.

I came to understand this reading Annie Ernaux. In *Happening*, she writes: 'Now I know that this ordeal and this sacrifice were necessary for me to want to have children.'

I fully believe it's a boy, a winter baby, born thirty years ago, who allowed me to be free, to be by turns a student, traveller, lover, wife, mother, reader, tourist, journalist, and writer.

With these few words, I am finally ready to reveal your absence.

Thanks to the Veil Law, your absence is not the result of hours of cruelty, mistreatment, blood, fear, humiliation, and contempt.

I did not do it with a 'lightness of heart'; it was neither comfortable, nor convenient, nor banal. I was neither in distress nor in a state of high drama, but that spring of 1984 was, I understand now, 'an extreme human experience, bearing on life and death, time, law, ethics, and taboo' (Annie Ernaux, *Happening*).

I CAN FINALLY WRITE IT: your absence has accompanied me for thirty years.

Your absence liberated me, and made me the woman I am today.

FRIENDSHIP

In memory of my friend Emmanuelle
(1966–2018)

There are only people who 'pass away' and
are no longer talked about – maybe they will
be talked about later, once we have forgotten
that they are dead. Death has become
unnamable.

> —PHILIPPE ARIÈS, *Essays on the History of*
> *Death*
> *in the West from the Middle Ages to the Present*

One of the greatest hazards in life is the
family you are born into.

> —EMMANUEL FARHI (1978–2000)

August 2018

Héloïse has stayed in Paris all summer long, though she is no longer receiving treatment.

Colombe has just come back from two weeks in Patmos, where she has swum, read, shed a few tears about her love life, and generally had an excellent time.

Héloïse has this way of looking you straight in the eye and speaking clearly, without beating around the bush.

She says to Colombe, I'm not going to make it.

Colombe doesn't know what to say.

Héloïse says, I'm going to die.

Colombe still cannot think what to say.

Héloïse says, I'm scared.

Colombe stammers, I hope you're going to get better, even though she knows her friend is not going to get better. The waiter arrives, Héloïse declares that she's hungry and would like oysters. Colombe has lost her appetite. She lies to Héloïse again, tells her the reason she is not hungry is because she ate something before coming out, not because of what her friend has just told her.

Héloïse orders. She is smiling, polite, efficient, as if death were not dining with them.

She asks for a glass of Pouilly-Fuissé. She knows the difference between a good wine and a wine that wants you to think it is good. Colombe, on the other hand, can get them confused.

Héloïse has a confession to make to her friend. Her face lights up. It's about her ex-husband. Really? Yes. They're talking again, they've been spending hours on the phone. Do they see each other? No, he doesn't dare, but they chat about music, the children, everything. She still loves him, she wonders if they might ever get together again. It's true, he never comes to see her, he's probably scared of her illness, but she's never bored with him. He has just split up with his latest girlfriend. Colombe nods, yes, it could be worth a go.

Colombe is hungry now, she eats Héloïse's oysters and asks,

—What about your lover, the one who's actually around, who doesn't just call you, the one you told me takes you in his arms and looks at you for hours? No man has ever adored you like that. They had only been together for a fortnight when he found out she was ill, and he has remained unblinking, doting, and stalwart throughout.

He has been to Lourdes to pray.

—I'd have preferred it if he'd stayed here.

The lover is a believer.

—The miracles of Lourdes are real, I have proof, Colombe hears herself say.

And she makes up a story about a woman who was cured of a fatal disease at Lourdes.

Héloïse and Colombe compare the ex-husband and the lover, weighing up the pros and cons. Her lover is wonderful. Colombe is in favour of him. Héloïse agrees, her lover is wonderful, she loves him, he is generous, he has never flinched from her fatal disease.

Héloïse orders chocolate profiteroles and remarks on a man at another table, a regular at this café. He is a writer (the café, the Select, is in the 6th arrondissement and thus, of course, frequented by writers). The writer has never so much as glanced at Colombe, who also frequents the Select, which vexes her. He looks directly at Héloïse, visibly charmed, and she blushes.

Héloïse giggles, she likes the look of the stranger, she smiles at him.

Héloïse wants to know everything Colombe knows about the man.

Colombe looks him up on her phone.

Héloïse lets Colombe finish her dish of profiteroles, Colombe realises she hasn't touched them. Héloïse has a stomachache. She wants to go home.

As soon as she gets home, Héloïse calls Colombe.

Colombe is worried when she sees Héloïse's number flash up, she should have walked her back.

But Héloïse just wants to talk to her about the guy in the café.

—He's so cute, what's his name again? A writer. Is it any good, what he writes? Would I like it? I've never dated a writer. Do you think he'd like me?

Colombe tells her yes, he certainly looked very charmed,

but doesn't elaborate on what she thought of the writer as a potential boyfriend for Héloïse.

—It's easy, he's there every night, we can go back whenever you like.

Héloïse doesn't see the writer again. She dies a fortnight later.

Héloïse and Colombe met when they were eleven years old. It was this subject, love – more than politics, more than global warming, more than the future of the planet – that they talked about most when they were together. They weren't cool or politically engaged, they were two girls on a quest for love.

1977

When it comes to the wealthy and the bourgeois, people think they already know, like they do with pigs,* that they don't like them.

Bourgeois: narrow-minded, according to an excellent dictionary of synonyms. Bourgeois: ordinary; bourgeois: conformist, conventional, selfish, rude, dull, mediocre, average, slippery, philistine, unoriginal, superficial; bourgeois: vulgar.

The bourgeois are miserable, and it is their own fault. Always moaning about their rich people's problems: their depression, their diets, the work they're having done in their apartments, the dust, their maids, the queue for the chairlifts. Bourgeois

---

*A reference to Jacques Brel's 1968 song 'Les Bourgeois' whose chorus goes: 'The middle class are just like pigs / The older they get, the dumber they get / The middle class are just like pigs / The fatter they get, the less they regret.'

women are invariably inhibited, sexually frustrated, their skin too taut, their feet crammed into high heels, their hands gripping their handbags. And what about their children, particularly their daughters? No hope there either.

Colombe and Héloïse have known each other since they were eleven, they were in the same class at the famous École Alsacienne, a private school for Parisian bourgeois liberals — the worst kind, the ones who have all the luck and none of the rules, who think they're on the right side of history because they are left-wing and that means they can't be accused of being bourgeois. Scum.

Colombe and Héloïse are daddy's girls, rich kids born with silver spoons in their mouths, with their sunglasses, connections, internships, agnès b. T-shirts. For a long time that's all they know about life. They should be made to suffer like everyone else. They should be locked up. They should be humiliated, belittled. They should have to go through what every little girl, every teenager, every woman in the world suffers, there's no reason they should escape their fate just because they were born in the right neighborhood.

Why Héloïse and Colombe and not us?

Well, you only need to look at their mothers, who might be forty but don't look a day over thirty, with their smooth skin, maintained with delicately scented Guerlain face cream, their manicured nails, their stomachs free of stretch marks despite their pregnancies. They reign like queens over their children's lives. The kiss they grant them before they go out to dinner. Look inside their closets: a succession of silk blouses on wooden hangers, arranged according to colour and ironed by other women not as lucky as they are. See how they fill their refrigerators: homemade chocolate mousse in glass pots, with none of those disgusting carcinogenic additives, the tiniest petits pois that require a person to be paid to shell them by hand, coffee beans, with an incomparable flavour, to be ground in a special machine a few minutes before being served.

You only need to see Héloïse and Colombe reading in their own bedrooms — they don't have to share with anyone — with walls covered in floral fabrics from Laura Ashley, books they don't have to return to the library, peace and quiet — they are never disturbed by shouting from a neighbouring apartment — the sheets on their bed, plain, crisp percale with matching pillows, their pink-and-white candy-striped cotton underwear, the pale, pristine carpet, they can get up in the night and they won't get cold feet, their tartan wool robes and red leather slippers, the miniature perfume bottles they collect, their Wednesday schedules, dance class, horseback riding, English, piano, Chinese, their Saturday schedules, drawing, drama, tennis, swimming. They get taken to the opera, to the Comédie-Française, to the Museum of Modern Art, but never to shopping malls; they have summer holidays and winter holidays, and even the boring October and Easter holidays, when it almost always rains, are not boring for Colombe and Héloïse, they have classes to perfect the way they bend their knees on skis, their grip on their tennis rackets, their British accents, their knowledge of the Italian Renaissance.

They are eleven years old and they have already visited Italy, Spain, and America but they have never been to the USSR, anywhere in Eastern Europe, or a campsite.

.   .   .

THE SUMMER OF 1977, Colombe spends a week with her parents on Porquerolles, a tiny island off the south coast of France where holidayers get around by bicycle. Their hotel, a large old manor house clad in salmon-pink render, is located on an isolated part of the island. Guests are picked up from the port in a red Dodge driven by an Egyptian man dressed in white. The regulars greet him, shake his hand, know him by name. Ahmed smiles. He handles the open truck with panache. It's the kind that transports agricultural workers, except that it's been fitted with two comfortable leather benches, and the guests cling to the side bars, conscious of their privilege. It is one of the very few cars authorised here, and they are not used to this kind of transport. The Dodge sets off down a track pocked with red rocks that skirts a forest of eucalyptus trees. The entire island is a protected nature reserve. The hotel is surrounded by a large garden of umbrella pines and oleanders, in whose shade have been placed heavy white swinging chairs with navy blue canvas cushions. Colombe's room, small and white with a dark wood bed and a white quilted coverlet, has neither its own bathroom nor toilet. She is astonished, but her father says, that's the whole point of this place, its faded charm. After this first visit, they will return there every summer; her mother writes to the hotel as early as January, hoping to book two rooms despite the waiting list. One winter, the owners decide to renovate the manor house, turn it into a soulless pink palace. It is no longer to their taste, so they go instead to Port-Cros, the neighbouring island, to another hotel, of similarly faded charm, with the same simple rooms, cramped bathrooms, regulars who greet each other silently with a nod, the same small coves and deserted beaches where people go running in the morning before breakfast. You need nothing more than a sarong, you never have to search for a shady spot to park the car, or to lug your picnic, folding chairs, and umbrellas, or to fall asleep in full sun, your body sticky and itching from seawater and sun cream. You just walk a few steps and settle down in a canvas deck chair under the umbrella pines and go for another swim in the golden early evening light. That summer of 1977 Colombe acquires a taste for swimming in the Mediterranean, where she knows only empty beaches, the luxury of what appears — because it is protected from those who do not have money — to be wild and untamed.

When she disembarks from the boat in Toulon or Hyères, Colombe looks around at the pizzerias, the swimsuit stores, the parking spaces and campsites, the supermarkets and traffic circles, the crowds. She shields herself from guilt by telling herself that the splendor of the sparkling water, its perfect coolness in perfect balance with the perfect heat of the air, the delicious gratification of a gleaming, salty body, is a drug that is both pure and free. She mustn't leave its depths, she must stay like that, without coming back down to earth, the site of all the social contingencies that she so rarely comes up against.

When Héloïse tells her all about her holiday in Saint-Tropez, her grandmother's house, and days spent at Club 55, Colombe thinks how much luckier other people are than she is.

.   .   .

IN OCTOBER 1977, Héloïse and Colombe go on a school trip to la Grande Borne, a new neighborhood in Grigny, a suburb south of Paris. They take the suburban train from Luxembourg station, the one nearest to where they live. The brand-new red, white, and blue carriages, the lawns surrounding the towers, the outdoor playground, the sculptures in the form of coloured snakes, the portrait of Rimbaud, the colours on the walls, light blue, red, yellow, they love it all. Colombe thinks she would like to live there, in a modern building, rather than a gloomy old building in Paris.

You can hate them for not seeing. It's easy, and it will happen, and they will be punished, especially Héloïse.

LET US IMAGINE a sociologist with sharp observation skills has been commissioned to undertake research on the Parisian bourgeoisie of the 1970s, and to that end has been installed simultaneously in the homes of Héloïse's and Colombe's parents. The sociologist, a feminist from a working-class background, has a degree from the University of Vincennes. She begins her study with a description of the two apartments and their inhabitants, initially assuming them to be virtually identical, before realising her mistake.

Two apartments near the Luxembourg Gardens, with parquet floors, marble fireplaces, ceiling mouldings (cherubs, fleur-de-lys), galley kitchens, and bathrooms with brightly coloured tiles and fittings (ochre, apple green), the living and dining rooms separated by French doors (which were removed by Colombe's parents on the advice of an interior designer who told them they needed to open up the space, let the air circulate), the same mix of antique furniture (inherited, in the case of Héloïse's parents, picked up at flea markets or from antique dealers in the case of Colombe's) and contemporary pieces (understated Italian design at Héloïse's, austere Danish at Colombe's).

This is all they have ever known. Colombe's grandmothers live in smaller apartments, with one bedroom, a living room, and a dining room, but that makes sense, thinks Colombe, they live alone.

Their classmates from the École Alsacienne hold birthday parties in apartments with exactly the same layout. Only the décor is different. Some are extravagantly colourful, with fuchsia, bright orange, and lemon-yellow flowered wallpaper, plastic furniture, and squishy pouffes, others are furnished with straight-backed chairs upholstered in dark green velvet and engravings of ducks on the walls.

To begin with, the sociologist thinks she can distinguish between these different families by their decorative choices:

1. Families with flamboyant wallpaper are left-wing, prefer goat's cheese to Camembert, the fathers (and sometimes the mothers) are professionals or intellectuals. They declare themselves to be 'anti-bourgeois', because to be bourgeois is to be conformist, and they are not.

2. Families with sofas upholstered in dark green or beige velvet are comfortable with who they are, for

them bourgeois is not an insult, it's fine. They tend
to be right-wing.

But after a while she starts to wonder if perhaps these crite-
ria are a little simplistic.

The building where Colombe's parents have their apartment, with its long hallway and small kitchen, was constructed
at the end of the nineteenth century. Colombe's parents clearly
belong to category 1: comfortable in their social class, with
shiny gold wallpaper in the foyer, silver in the dining room.
The prospect of an alliance between the Socialist party and
the Communist party does not alarm them. The sociologist
suspects Colombe's father of having been a communist student
activist, to start with she rather takes to him, before changing
her mind and concluding he is a traitor for having chosen such
a bourgeois lifestyle. She swallows her judgement; she owes it
to herself to remain neutral.

The sociologist articulates the word bourgeois and watches
for the respondent's reaction. She has just taken a course on
nonverbal communication. Is he shocked (signified by a frown,
pursed lips, an angry look on his face, twitchiness), or is he,
rather, amused?

The mothers are not asked this type of question, it is not on
the questionnaire (she did once bring this up in a meeting, but
the head of department didn't hear).

Instead, she asks the women about the functioning of the
household. Colombe's mother appears utterly uninterested in
the question, and always slightly misses the point. She has a
full-time housekeeper who does the vacuuming, ironing, clean-

ing, shopping and cooking, while she takes care of the rest, making sure everything runs smoothly. She pays for this help out of her salary.

Héloïse's parents' apartment is on the top floor of a seventeenth-century *hôtel particulier* on an elegant street just south of the Luxembourg Gardens. It has high ceilings, and honey-coloured herringbone parquet whose oak slats are an inch wider than those in Colombe's parents' apartment. No green velvet or antique engravings, as the sociologist has been expecting. The white walls are hung with portraits (she wonders if they are ancestors) and modern paintings, bright splashes of colour. The children are baptised but have not taken their first communion.

The entire building belongs to one of Héloïse's great-aunts. She has no children. Succession and inheritance are serious topics and are certainly not to be discussed with anyone outside the family.

The sociologist is not immediately able to distinguish between Colombe's and Héloïse's social milieux. She sees wealthy, bourgeois families, large apartments, two parents, one daughter, almost identical fathers (short, corpulent, balding, cheerful, white-collar professionals, Héloïse's father is a notary and the son of a notary, Colombe's is a doctor, the son of a tailor who spoiled his children rotten) and almost identical mothers (beautiful, distant, uptight, university educated). She notes the physical resemblance between Héloïse and Colombe, they dress in the same way, clogs, overalls, culottes, Shetland sweaters, their mothers never buy them expensive clothes, but everything is well-made and at least one size up, made to last; they both have light brown shoulder-length hair, often tangled, hastily tied back in a ponytail, Colombe's hair is never smooth and gets very knotted because she forgets to brush it (she no longer has a nanny to help her get ready in the morning); Héloïse is better-groomed (her mother makes sure nothing is out of place).

When she looks a little more closely, however, the sociologist realises that, from a strictly anthropological point of view, there are significant differences between these two young ladies of the post-1968 bourgeoisie.

Héloïse has been taught to use a butter knife to help herself to a slice of butter, which must be placed not directly on the bread, but onto a small plate, and she must then use her own knife to spread the butter on the bread. Colombe sees no problem in plunging her own knife into the pretty silver ramekin brought back from the Silver Vaults in London, then spreading it straight onto her bread, and the same with the jam. In other words, she is charming, but her manners leave something to be desired. Neither her mother nor her father has ever insisted she say please, madame, thank you, madame, or punished her if she does not. Rather than a proper bourgeois upbringing, she has had guidance from the cleaner, Madame Simone, about being kind and attentive to others. Later, Colombe will inherit from her parents a decorative silver prong to be clamped over a leg of lamb to hold it in place while the meat is being carved at the table, a plate decorated with entwined purple and pale green asparagus on which sits a matching dish with slits in it to drain asparagus, an elegant silver tube to hold nutmeg with its own tiny silver scraper to flavour soups with the spice, dessert spoons, ivory-handled fish knives, but she will still eat with her mouth open and make chewing sounds, while Héloïse is perfectly behaved at the table, handles her silverware with dexterity, knows when to hold her tongue, sends thank-you notes even when she has merely been invited for tea, and writes sensitive letters of condolence to people she barely knows.

Héloïse's parents belong to the *grande bourgeoisie*, and her mother is descended from the aristocracy, while Colombe's social class is indeterminate (her grandparents were Jewish immigrants from Eastern Europe whose children benefited from an excellent public education).

Later, Héloïse will accept that she is bourgeois, that is simply how it is, there is nothing to apologise for. Her father leaves for work at 7 a.m. and returns home at 9 p.m. There are rules to obey, she has to achieve excellence, so she makes herself do it, studies diligently. Héloïse suffers the disadvantages of a bourgeois education and its obligations. She knows how to behave. Her parents demand a great deal from her, and she hopes to live up to their expectations.

She spends half of every holiday doing something useful: she goes to England to learn English and Germany to learn German, she goes to tennis and sailing camp, even maths camp. It never occurs to her to do nothing, not to be learning something.

Colombe, who prefers illusion to reality, will take years to admit that her parents are rich (well, not particularly rich, but richer than average), money does not interest her, she never talks about it or seeks it out. This indifference is the very proof that she is bourgeois: you have to have money to believe that money doesn't matter. Colombe insists on the fact that her four immigrant grandparents arrived in France with nothing. When her parents die, she will inherit furniture and even enough money to buy a small apartment in Paris, but bourgeois, that derogatory label? No, not at all.

AFTER THE SOCIOLOGIST interviews the two girls, she summarises their situation as follows:

They have never gone hungry.

Colombe has an account at the bakery, where she may ask for whatever she wants.

Héloïse has a snack waiting for her on a tray when she gets home from school. A glass of fruit juice and a piece of buttered baguette with four little squares of chocolate.

They think their life is normal, average, just like that of lots of other French people, neither better nor worse.

When she was younger, Colombe even used to wonder if she was a bit common. At lunch at a friend's house one day, the mother asked what her surname was, then what her mother's maiden name was, she shook her head from left to right, no, she had never heard of either family, she even went to check in *Who's Who*, nothing.

At eleven, they are both still relatively unaware of their social position; they look at themselves in the mirror – middle class, upper class, there is no difference that they can see.

Colombe asked her father, what are we? Are we rich or are we normal?

He replied, we're average.

They tell the sociologist that they know how lucky they are, not that anyone has ever told them they are, but they have read books like *Little Good-for-Nothing*, with unhappy children and strict schoolteachers who hand out lots of homework and beat their pupils with a cane. Which is really not their case.

They talk a lot about their school.

Their teachers at the École Alsacienne don't give homework, the students have to hand in a 'magnum opus' once a term, an original piece of work that they have worked on intensively. Héloïse invents crossword puzzles, charades, and board games, and Colombe writes and illustrates stories. They are not expected to learn things by heart, in case they are traumatised and develop a phobia for school or, worse, find it boring.

Colombe is disorganised and idle, Héloïse conscientious and serious. The sociologist notes 'the very worst injustice': in an ordinary school, Colombe would likely be 'oriented' toward a trade school if she did not get her act together and start studying. But because she is from this new social class that emerged in the 1970s, the left-wing-intellectual-liberal-bourgeois class, she is instead encouraged and supported, and will end up at a good university.

The interviewer, in spite of not having had such opportunities herself, is neither bitter nor envious; she thinks: *good for her.*

SHE MAY THUS CONCLUDE that the end of the twentieth century saw the arrival of a new bourgeois class, born of the 1968 revolution, ready to enjoy all the perks of their social advancement without any of the disadvantages.

1978

They look like each other, short, slight, brown hair, pale skin, light eyes, and this resemblance is one of the foundations of their friendship.

They wish they were taller, they have a bit of a complex about it, how many inches would it take to make them feel more self-confident? They hope to grow a little more, and also to be allowed to buy dresses and sandals and dance cheek to cheek with boys who are in love with them.

They aren't cool; the others – the ones who dress well, are good at skateboarding, just a few months away from smoking cigarettes – don't know their names, or they get them mixed up, they're Héloïse and Colombe, *les petites*, late developers, hauling bulky bags with their riding and dance gear, they come out of school on Rue d'Assas and stop at the bakery for an almond croissant. They go up Rue des Chartreux without stopping at the café Le Chartreux because they don't play pinball, don't drink coffee, don't know how to talk to boys with a detached air, don't giggle with them. When they walk past the window they can't help looking in. Who is sitting on the ban-

quettes with a view of the wall painted with a blue Vesuvius?
Who is glued to a stool at the bar? The big kids. Eighth graders.

They walk past the Petit Luxembourg, Héloïse will turn
left towards the Grand Luxembourg, Colombe the other way
towards the Avenue de l'Observatoire, but first, because they
have things to talk about, they sit down on a bench. Facing
them are beds of yellow and red tulips, an avenue of chestnut
trees with large green leaves casting shade, grass like plush
upholstery, Carpeaux's fountain and its flamboyant bronze
horses spouting jets of water that freeze when it is spectacu-
larly cold, a sight that always impresses them. These bronze
statues, these huge trees, these trimmed lawns, these yellow
and red tulips are their background decor, they are not blasé,
their parents have shown them how beautiful it all is, they
admire it, but they are used to seeing beauty around them.

There's that birthday party at a new kid's house, a boy who
hasn't been at their school since kindergarten like they have.
Tom is American and has a sprinkling of freckles on his snub
nose. Sporty Héloïse wears coloured suede Kickers boots, and
Colombe, who is still a bit of a goody two-shoes, Start-Rite
from England, whose style, season after season, never changes.
Vanessa Djian wears ballet pumps from Sacha in royal blue
with yellow stars, or Stan Smiths, sometimes even cowboy-
boots – of course, she has been invited to Tom's house, and it is
easy to see why Héloïse and Colombe have not. In winter, they
are given the choice between Mary Janes with one buckle or
two, in one of two colours navy or red; in summer, they wear
open-toed shoes with crepe soles from the Cendrine boutique

on Rue Vavin, where a woman with white hair clipped into a high white chignon bends over their small feet, measures them, presses her thumb hard on the new leather by their toes, checking that the shoe is supportive and their feet won't be cramped, that it is not too narrow and will fit them for at least six months, nor too wide, or they could trip and hurt themselves; it's a serious ceremony that excludes in advance the ballet pumps and cowboy boots, parties, and making out that they can only dream of. And yet, when Colombe goes to bed – her new shoes with their sugary leather smell on the floor by her bed, navy blue like a chic young lady, almost the same as her mother's moccasins, the cardboard box lined with tissue paper that she asked if she could keep – she tells herself that, thanks to them, a new life is about to begin.

1978

They are never sick. They catch colds, scrape their knees, graze their arms, have tummy aches, get fevers of 100 degrees, once as high as 102, the pediatrician comes and lays his cool hands on their temples, they are vaccinated and have braces so their teeth are perfect, they go to the ophthalmologist, have physiotherapy, are treated and mollycoddled, their spines and feet are as straight as their teeth and eyesight, nothing is forgotten, nothing is neglected or left to chance, nothing is so minor that it 'doesn't matter', nothing is allowed to be wonky or crooked, they are perfect.

At the beginning of fifth grade, because Héloïse's summer holiday was so much more interesting than hers, Colombe tells her best friend that she had meningitis over the summer and almost went blind. After she read Helen Keller's autobiography *The Story of My Life*, in which Keller describes how she escaped her solitude through sheer willpower, Colombe drew a causal link between Keller's genius and the meningitis that caused her to go deaf. She thought, *If I say I had meningitis, Héloïse will think I'm a genius like Helen Keller.*

Héloïse never tells lies and can't imagine anyone lying to her.

1978

A photograph taken for an assignment on Roman antiquity in preparation for a school trip to Rome: they are wearing white panties and draped in white sheets, sitting in a large planter. The planter is meant to be a Roman bath.

On the school trip they go to the Forum, all they can talk about is Valerie and Frédéric, who kissed on the mouth the day before, they dart behind the columns to try to catch them kissing again, but in fact they never go anywhere near one another, they are totally ignoring each other. Valerie, spotting Frédéric from a distance, laughs and talks loudly, and Frédéric turns his back on her.

1979

The week after the end of the Christmas holiday, Héloïse and Colombe both overhear their parents having the same conversation and they are very troubled.

Héloïse and Colombe eavesdrop on their parents talking about Simone de Beauvoir and Jean-Paul Sartre as a model couple; they hear the same expressions, 'free love', 'necessary love and contingent love', 'fidelity is an obsolete notion', 'a prison for the petit bourgeois', quite as if this were a normal topic of conversation, a theoretical discussion for children to listen to, a learning process, a key part of their education, as if this revelation represented the ideal of a happy and fulfilled life. On the one hand there are wives and husbands, their parents; on the other, men and women with whom their parents can have sexual relationships (though this word, *sexual*, is not uttered).

'That's disgusting!' they exclaim, grimacing.

Héloïse swears to Colombe that her parents love each other, she knows they do. The proof: her father puts his hand on her mother's shoulder and tells her she is beautiful, and her mother looks at her father as if he were God.

—Why are they talking like this? Because it's fashionable? Have they been reading some book? Did they watch a discussion on television?

COLOMBE, on the other hand, has figured out that her father is cheating on her mother (she has no proof, but she is sure of it).

Her mother loves her father, but does her father love her mother? Is this thing of quoting Sartre and Beauvoir as if he has finally found a solution to all his problems simply a way to cheat on her mother without guilt?

AT THIRTEEN, they become their fathers' vigilant wives, rummaging through their jacket pockets, sniffing for perfume on their shirts, peeking at their diaries. Together, they make the decision to confront their respective fathers.

Colombe has prepared her speech: her father has got to choose his family, because 'you can't have your cake and eat it, you know.' Her father listens, then lowers his *Nouvel Observateur* and replies dryly that it is none of her business.

Héloïse lets it go. She agrees with her friend's father, it's none of their business and her parents love each other, she is sure of it. Her confidence irritates Colombe.

THEY TALK ABOUT LOVE.

Will either of them ever have a lover? Will he be blond or dark-haired? Will he be rich? What will he do for a living? Will they get married? In the countryside? In Paris? In a long dress or a short dress? How many children will they have?

Let's hope that the Sartre-Beauvoir model will have gone out of fashion by the time they grow up.

They swear to each other that they will be different from their parents, they are positive they will, their relationships will be 'normal and happy', they declare on the way to school. They haven't yet swapped their backpacks for the leather satchels with a rope strap from Upla they dream of, because their parents don't want to spoil them and think that a shoulder bag with a strap would be bad for their backs, whereas their carefully chosen backpacks are much more appropriate while they are still growing.

WHILE AWAITING THEIR longed-for Upla satchels and their future weddings, they are growing up together, which is to say they are not growing very much. They are still the smallest in the class, two skinny girls with little bottoms and tiny breasts that no boy ever looks at.

They think the fact that they are rarely invited to parties is proof they are not physically attractive. They have the same light eyes — Héloïse's are blue, Colombe's green — chestnut hair, regular features, narrow noses. For their social class this is quite normal, thinks the sociologist — generations of good marriages, healthy food, and holidays in the mountains have forged their regular, reassuring, slim physiques.

She is mistaken. About Colombe, anyway.

COLOMBE HAS NEVER been to any of the countries where her grandparents were born, she only knows there are walnut trees in Transylvania and they eat walnut cake there like at her paternal grandmother's house, and in Bessarabia they drink very sweet tea poured from a samovar like at her maternal grandmother's house, but it would never occur to anyone to go there on holiday.

Colombe's parents rent houses for their summer holidays or go to hotels, there is no family summer house, no village, no roots.

HÉLOÏSE SPENDS the whole month of July at her maternal grandmother's château in the Basque country, where her mother spent all her summers when she was a child, the wallpaper in the bathroom hasn't changed, nor has the order and frugality of the menus, the pâté and hard-boiled eggs every day for lunch, the cold terra-cotta tiles in the wide hallway leading to the children's bedrooms, the part of the beach in Saint-Jean-de-Luz where they have a canvas beach hut, the surnames of the people they visit. One day Héloïse was summoned by her grandmother, who explained to her how many sheets of toilet paper it is acceptable to use.

In August, Héloïse goes to stay with her paternal grandmother in Saint-Tropez, a house in the Ponche port, purchased in 1951 thanks to the family of her husband, a naval officer based in Toulon. She comes back with enough to talk about until Christmas.

IT IS THIS DIFFERENCE that finally allows Colombe to understand that there is an absence of place and history in her family, and that there's something off about this absence. The stories Héloïse recounts about her family are linked in different ways to the history of France. On her mother's side one of Henry of Navarre's mistresses, a priest beheaded during the Revolution, an officer in Napoleon's army, an emigrant who made his fortune in Mexico, a general who died in the First World War, leaving his widow to raise five children alone, a flamboyant aristocrat refusing to abandon his ramshackle château. On her father's side, a childhood in Provence, a great-grandfather who was a naval officer, a grandmother who inherited a large candied-fruit company, thirty-two hectares of vineyards in the Var, names, places, houses, *cousinhood*, a new word Colombe had never heard before, family trees with no broken branches. Colombe reads the phone book to try to find some relatives.

1979

Héloïse's mother wants to put her name down for a *rallye*, a debutante ball, organised by one of her cousins. 'It's the ideal opportunity to make contacts, widen your social circle, meet other young people from good families. You meet up one Saturday a month to learn to dance. You'll see, it's terrific fun. Then, once you're fifteen, there are lots of grand parties. We'll buy you a lovely taffeta dress.' She won't take no for an answer. 'It's important,' she says. When Héloïse refuses she is furious.

'I'd never go to that kind of thing, and what's more I'd be the only one from the École Alsacienne. No one goes to them anymore, everyone would think I was so square. They're for idiots,' Héloïse tells Colombe, who thinks to herself she would love it if her parents made her go (but they probably don't even know what it is). Colombe loves dancing and getting dressed up. She thinks she's shallow, and admires her friend's integrity, her refusal to be bought a taffeta dress to go dancing with boys in black tie.

1979

Héloïse always wears overalls and culottes and can shimmy up a rope all the way to the ceiling of the gymnasium at the École Alsacienne. It's impressive to watch, arm, leg, arm, leg, one after the other, apparently effortless, never stopping or hesitating, looking not down at the ground but up to the top of the rope where the knot meets the ceiling beam, six metres above the ground. When she reaches the top she condescends to look down at everyone sitting on the floor, then shimmies back down with equal agility. The gymnastics teacher congratulates her, she smiles. She sits down next to Colombe, shoots her a sidelong glance, waits for her to say something.

Colombe is so jealous she turns away. *Sorry, I wasn't watching.* She would rather die than acknowledge Héloïse's feat.

It's Colombe's turn now. The smooth rope is unthinkable, she goes straight to the knotted rope. Héloïse encourages her, which makes Colombe want to hit her. She dashes forward, knowing full well what will happen, yet hoping that this time it will be different, she has grown, she's got more strength in her arms, she's been watching the way Héloïse focuses on the rope, unaware that Colombe is studying her every move so she can copy her. She makes it look so easy, one arm, one leg, one arm, one leg. Colombe's left hand clutches the rope, it's too thick, her fingers don't go round it, she squeezes with all her might, her palm is burning. She wedges her left foot onto the first knot that touches the ground, rolls her right leg around the rope, she's wearing shorts and feels the slide of the hemp against her skin, she picks up her left foot to try to place it on top of the second knot, eight inches off the ground, it slips, she pretends not to notice, lifts her right foot and places it on the left one, the hemp has tiny barbs that prick her skin but don't keep her from slipping, she is getting nowhere, her feet are entwined so it looks like she can do the same as Héloïse, but the only thing that is a few centimetres off the ground is her left toe pressed against the knot, her heel is pushing back and dragging down her whole body. She lifts her right foot again, with a little jump places it above her left foot, one leg on top of the other, heaves up her suddenly leaden buttocks, agonisingly gets past the first knot on the rope, she's done it, she is ninety centimetres off the ground, it's only her bottom dragging her down now, she can hear Héloïse cheering her on (surely she's making fun of her, getting her revenge, she must have noticed Colombe's refusal to acknowledge her achievement), she's made it to the second knot now, this has never happened before, she must be 120 centimetres off the ground, she dips her head down towards the wooden floor, feels dizzy, her legs are all twisted up and she can't move anymore, she's stuck, she can't go up and she can't go down, the hemp is burning the skin of her thighs and her calves, her palms are hot, she wants to cry. She is eleven years old, then twelve, thirteen, fourteen, fifteen, sixteen, seventeen, the same gym, the same rope, no progress, the second knot will be Colombe's unequalled feat. She drops to the floor, bruising her bottom and twisting her ankle. She wants Héloïse's admiration, not her pity. Humiliated, Colombe wants Héloïse to disappear from her sight forever.

1980

Héloïse and Colombe are fourteen, they are allowed to leave school at lunchtime. It must be March, the pale yellow sun announces the end of winter, and Héloïse bursts into tears, which never happens when she's with Colombe.

They are standing a little apart from the others, on the corner of Rue d'Assas and Rue Michelet, outside a large, high-end grocery store selling canned food with labels designed to appear handwritten. Colombe turns towards the window, embarrassed, then back to face Héloïse.

Héloïse tells her, 'It's the sun, it reminds me of being in Saint-Tropez with my grandmother.'

Colombe takes a few steps back, says nothing, and they join the others heading towards the Luxembourg Gardens or the bakery, she doesn't remember where they went next, but she does remember Héloïse lit up by the sun, her tears, her grandmother's tall, narrow house, the roof terrace planted with jasmine, her pink bathroom, her Opium perfume that seems so un-grandmotherly, Héloïse's grandmother, the very definition of love.

She has always been amazed that a grandmother could look

like Héloïse's, with her white trouser suits and matching pumps, pink lipstick, and most of all the things she teaches Héloïse that Héloïse later repeats to Colombe.

She tells her how beautiful she is.

She shows her how to smudge plum-coloured eyeshadow on her eyelids to bring out her blue eyes.

She adjusts the belt on Héloïse's dress, pulling it as tightly as she can.

She gives her a pair of silver-sequinned high-heeled sandals and tells her it doesn't matter if her feet hurt. What matters is how she looks.

She advises her to eat almonds if she wants large breasts.

She tells Héloïse that men are going to fall at her feet, and one day, like her, she will meet the man of her dreams, the most loving, brilliant husband, and she will be as happy as her grandmother was with Papy.

SHE COMES TO PARIS, peers into Colombe's eyes, then Héloïse's, and says that her granddaughter's eyes are more beautiful than her friend's, and of course Colombe understands.

HÉLOÏSE COMES HOME every summer from Saint-Tropez with clothes her grandmother has given her.

Not the clothes of a little girl or a well-bred teenager, no overalls from New Man or scarves from Benetton, no Liberty-print dresses from Cacharel or crepe-soled sandals from Start-

Rite. No normal stuff in blue, red, green, pink, grey. She comes home with a fuchsia pink Chanel jacket, a white Saint Laurent jacket with black buttons, a gold silk Hermès scarf, white Ferragamo pumps. Héloïse never wears any of them but she shows them, almost too hurriedly, to Colombe, who would very much like to try them on.

These are clothes that you never see anyone wearing, only in photographs in the kinds of magazines their mothers do not buy. Colombe's mother subscribes to the feminist magazine *F*, which doesn't publish the kind of fashion photography that 'demeans women' that Colombe loves. Héloïse's mother isn't interested in fashion, in things that don't last; she rarely buys clothes for herself and she wears the same thing every day, carefully chosen in the style of the British aristocracy – Shetland sweaters, twinsets, tweed skirts, everything very comfortable and sturdy.

Héloïse asks Colombe, do you think I can wear white pumps in Paris?

Colombe answers *of course*, secretly suspecting it would be a sartorial error and Héloïse will look so ridiculous she won't be invited to the American boy's party, which still grates.

Around the time she turns fourteen, Colombe goes up a few rungs on the ladder of cool; at last she is fashionable. Thanks to her father she wears ballet pumps from Sacha on her feet, Levi's 501s on her legs, and a grey and white sweatshirt over her shoulders.

This year she is invited to the American boy's party, but not Héloïse, who doesn't hide her disappointment. Colombe rubs it in, telling her how she got home at one in the morning, she kissed the American, he's her boyfriend, they're going out together.

It's time to goad Héloïse.

It's war between the two teenagers. Colombe has a new group of friends, Karin with her cowboy boots, Tom his denim jacket, Manu his Stan Smiths, and he plays tennis too. They go together to the very first McDonald's to open in Paris, on Boulevard Saint-Michel, with fake bookshelves on the walls.

Colombe is deeply invested in this fight, she is sure she will win, almost too easily. She doesn't realise that Héloïse isn't playing, the competition doesn't interest her.

In any case, Héloïse has a boyfriend now, his name is Philippe, he takes her to the cinema, and she seems to have forgotten Colombe as well.

1981

Something has happened in Héloïse's family, something to do with money.

Héloïse does not go to her grandmother's house for the Christmas holiday, but to Bali with her parents.

Her parents have bought a house in the Domaine du Cap near Saint-Tropez. They went back and forth about the purchase. The house has one big flaw. There is nowhere better than the Domaine du Cap, with its beautiful pre-war villas built by wealthy textile families from northern France. Such properties are passed down through the family. But the house they are considering buying is more recent, near the entrance of the Domaine in the area called Le Baou.

Having a house in Le Baou is a sign that one is not from one of the grand, storied families of the north. You are immediately identified as being 'new'. And that is a problem. Every time you say you have a house in Saint-Tropez, you find yourself having to justify it. *Where is it?* In the Domaine du Cap. *Wonderful, you must know the Thingamajigs. They have a house right at the very tip, are you near them?* Eyes lowered, you are forced to admit, 'Our house is in Le Baou.' The interlocutor will make of this what they will, undoubtedly aware of the difference between the families of the north, old money, and the families who got a great deal twenty years ago from a real estate developer with good taste. At the entrance to the Domaine, a warden asks visitors where they are going. Anyone who confesses they are only going to Le Baou is allowed in with a bored expression. No need to check or call the owners to make sure you're expected.

It's not a huge deal, but still. Héloïse's parents are used to being part of the ruling caste, with Basque aristocracy on her mother's side, and an old Provençal family on her father's. They consider themselves the elite, whether it's about taste, property, or membership. They decide to play the 'we're not snobs' card when they talk about this very minor defect: 'Yes, the house is in Le Baou, not that we care at all.' What they care about is the garden, with its arbutus, fig, plum, and lemon trees, that's why they chose the house. The previous owner was a bit of an eccentric, American, an artist with exquisite taste, a Mellon heiress.

EVERY TIME HÉLOÏSE wants to tell her about some breathtaking landscape she saw in Bali, Colombe abruptly changes the subject. She won't let Héloïse tell her about her holiday.

But she does accept an invitation to visit the new house during the February holiday.

It is built of candy-floss-pink concrete. You walk through a terraced garden overlooking the sea to get to the front door. Colombe stops in front of some small trees with long, thin, brown branches, she goes closer and sees lemons hanging off them. It is the first time that Colombe has seen lemons growing on a tree, she touches them incredulously, can't get over their size. She smells them, feels their weight in her hand, takes pictures of them. She is dazzled. She cries out, 'Lemon trees!' and strangely her jealousy evaporates.

Héloïse shows her the kitchen with its dumb waiter, rotisserie grill, deep fryer, ice cream maker, two refrigerators, a panel with bells with labels indicating the names of the rooms: the blue room, the pink room, the purple room, the small sitting room. They take an old-fashioned elevator with a gate and buttons marked mezzanine, second floor, third floor, fourth floor, they go all the way up to a large circular room with a white deep-pile carpet and a long, curved banquette that goes all round the walls, upholstered in fuchsia-pink Indian fabric. Colombe has never seen a house like this except in the Italian interiors magazines her father likes to buy. She opens an arched glass door that gives onto a terrace with a view of the sea, inhales the bracing air, then goes back inside.

They admire the tiled bathrooms, one entirely black, one lemon yellow, one candy pink, one turquoise. The house was built in the early 1960s, it's like going back in time. Colombe exclaims, 'It's like a film set or a game show.' Héloïse says nothing. She sleeps in a large room with a four-poster bed draped in white muslin. She has her own bathroom. Héloïse and Colombe quickly get used to this new house, it too becomes normal.

IN MAY, François Mitterrand is elected president of France, and Héloïse's parents are alarmed. They voted for the sitting president, Valéry Giscard d'Estaing. They once received a neighbourly invitation to coffee at the president's official holiday residence in Brégançon, a little farther down the coast, from Anne-Aymone, the president's wife. He even chatted to them for a few minutes when they arrived, which fuelled their dinner party conversations for over a year.

The question is, should they move to Switzerland? Héloïse tells this to Colombe, explaining that it's because of the communists who'll be in the government. Various parents of their school friends are appointed ministers. A friend of Héloïse's father studied with the president's chief of staff. This may come in useful should they one day find themselves in any kind of predicament.

Colombe's parents, on the other hand, voted for the socialists' and communists' joint slate, and they believe in paying taxes. It is only many years later that Colombe discovers they always held on to a small Swiss bank account.

1983

Héloïse spent the summer dancing the night away in Saint-Tropez clubs.

At the beginning of the school year, Colombe insists she tell her everything.

Héloïse met a twenty-six-year-old Italian called Matteo.

Colombe spent the summer at a sleepaway camp in Switzerland. She adores the place, the mountains, hiking in the nature reserve, paddling in the icy waters of the river, eating grilled sausages then Sugus candies for dessert, but she longs for Saint-Tropez.

At sunrise in Saint-Tropez, Matteo buys Héloïse a *pain au chocolat*, still warm from the oven, Matteo knows the baker, who opens up just for him, Matteo has rented a house in Rayol, it is just a few steps across the garden and through a gate to get to the beach. Matteo has dark eyes. At the end of the summer Matteo gives Héloïse a ring with a yellow stone. Matteo drives a red convertible. Matteo puts his arm around her shoulder when they walk. Matteo cries when the summer comes to an end.

Much later, when they are adults, Colombe asks Héloïse to tell her in as much detail as possible about Matteo and his convertible, the house on the water, Matteo's letters. Héloïse is surprised by Colombe's eagerness; it is the past, and though she still feels affection for Matteo, and has vaguely kept up with his news, she is in love with a different man now.

1984

Colombe comes home from school to hear that Madame Simone, their cleaner, has died in an accident. What exactly happened is unclear, something to do with an elevator, and Colombe daren't ask any questions.

Her father telephones and says, it's so sad, we are all so terribly sad.

Colombe goes to the funeral, she takes Madame Simone's son in her arms and holds him tight, he is the same age as her and she is meeting him for the first time, even though they live a hundred metres from each other.

Madame Simone is the first person she knows to die.

Until then, Colombe has been spared an encounter with death.

Colombe is seventeen, yet she does not understand she is never going to see Madame Simone again, that she will miss Madame Simone for years, will always regret not having asked her more about her life, not having listened to her, in the belief that she would always be there.

Thirty years after her death, Colombe can still taste the orange-blossom-and-chocolate cake Madame Simone used to make.

Madame Simone arrived every morning at eight o'clock sharp, prepared Colombe's breakfast — otherwise she wouldn't eat — opened all the bedroom windows, aired the beds (Colombe was meant to do this in her own room, but she never remembered). Then she filled a bucket with hot water and detergent, mopped the kitchen floor, wiped down the cupboards with a cloth soaked in white vinegar, vacuumed, and made the beds. By the time Colombe came home from school Madame Simone would be ironing, or sewing, or polishing the silverware, but she always got up to fix her a snack.

After Madame Simone's death, Colombe's cat stops eating and dies of grief.

1984

There are things that are expected of them, and things they hope for. Two teenage girls raised in the milieu of the Parisian intellectual bourgeoisie. Who could ask for more? It's the 1980s, François Mitterrand is president. The École Alsacienne, learning Chinese, an understanding of the importance of children having self-confidence, not too much homework, friends from the same milieu but also a few scholarship students selected for their intelligence and their capacity to work. School trips to Rome and Florence. Children should be happy, fulfilled, cultured, offered undreamed-of opportunities. The Luxembourg Gardens, the stunning avenues of pear trees, Swedish clogs from Kerstin Adolphson, leaves on the chestnut trees. Shelves laden with books they have read, the Veil Law legalising abortion. (Colombe has an abortion, it's completely fine.) On television they watch *Apostrophes* and Claude-Jean Philippe's *Ciné-club*. Cotton cardigans with snap fastenings and striped T-shirts from agnès b. at 180 francs a pop. Constant encouragement, projects, freedom of choice when it comes to what they are going to study at university. At seventeen, they go and see Chekhov's *The Cherry Orchard* at the Bouffes du Nord, directed by Peter Brook, which is where they find out it is possible to lose everything you thought was yours by right.

1984

Héloïse and Colombe pass their *baccalauréat*. They are not the first to do so in their families. It is perfectly normal.

Héloïse asks Colombe:

—Do you think you'll send your children to the school? (*The school*, that is, the École Alsacienne.)

—Oh no, I can't stand the neighbourhood, or the school, I'm going to send them to public school.

—I think I will. We've been happy there.

1985

After a year of preparatory classes in a private high school followed by a competitive examination, the names of those admitted to the highly selective university Sciences Po in Paris are posted in a window on Rue Saint-Guillaume. Héloïse sees her name, but Colombe does not see hers and she is disappointed, she tells herself there must have been a mistake. If

Héloïse has been admitted then she must have been, it is only logical. Colombe goes into the secretary's office to ask an assistant if they will be publishing another list in the course of the day. It seems natural to her to get what she wants. The astonished laughter of the assistant, the humiliation, transforms Colombe. She begins to work.

COLOMBE HAS A BOYFRIEND and Héloïse does not. Héloïse is nineteen and thinks she is never going to meet someone she really likes, a man who wants to get married and start a family.

Colombe has that kind of boyfriend, he is perfect, a definite possible future husband, studying at a top university, he plays tennis, owns a car, is good-looking and attentive.

Héloïse says, of course you have the perfect fiancé, you're so pretty, much prettier than I am.

Colombe does not see how having a boyfriend deserves any admiration.

She hadn't made any particular effort, it had happened so easily, this perfect young man, a friend's older brother, had caught her eye, and she his. They kissed, he is in love, and so is Colombe, at first.

Héloïse is envious of her, Colombe shrugs, love is easy, you just have to let it happen.

1988

A holiday snap shows them in bathing suits lounging on beach towels. They are twenty-two. They are both wearing gold clip-on earrings (they aren't the type to have pierced ears but they don't see why they shouldn't wear big earrings with a bathing suit).

Héloïse is looking confidently at the photographer, Colombe is watching her with affection. She is worried about Héloïse, she hopes things will work out for her, because she thinks Héloïse is so much nicer than she is. She is afraid that her friend will be taken advantage of, that people will abuse her trust.

But Colombe also finds Héloïse terribly conventional because she has told her she wants to join a golf club to meet a nice boy, and regrets having refused to go to debutante balls as a teenager. 'All the girls who went met such nice boys.' Colombe thinks she is a little boring because she has decided to go to business school. She tells Colombe, 'I have to earn a proper living' Colombe finds her too BCBG – too preppy and straight.*

Bon chic, bon genre ('well-dressed and well-heeled') is an expression used to refer to certain members of the Parisian upper classes, typically well-educated, well-connected, and descended from 'old money' families, preferably with some aristocratic ancestry. The phrase indicates a combination of a certain kind of fashionable but conventional taste with conservative notions of social respectability.

1989

They are on Hydra, posing for a photo on the backs of donkeys. They are on holiday with Colombe's father. He came down to the port to meet them, with a woman they don't know. They share a room and a four-poster bed at the Hotel Miranda, a white house filled with heavy wooden furniture and painted coffered ceilings. The shutters in their room are blocked by climbing jasmine. Breakfast — toast, honey, bitter coffee — is served in a courtyard planted with orange and lemon trees. They rent a boat for the day that takes them to a beach where there's no shade but they don't mind, the water in early September is warm, they stay there for hours, they eat tomato salads and almond croissants sprinkled with powdered sugar. The evening light is golden.

But all Colombe has held on to from that last holiday with her father is this photo of the two of them on donkeys, and her anger. This woman who has lodged herself between her father and her.

Colombe cannot recall a single uninterrupted conversation, or seeing her father in bathing trunks enjoying the sea and the sun, but she can still see this woman's face, this woman from Berlin with fine, delicate features, white-blond hair, linen clothes in shades of beige and cream, a son their age who tells them that his parents have just separated, well, his father has left his mother for another woman, his mother's relationship with Colombe's father is doing her a world of good. Colombe remains unmoved.

The following winter, Colombe's father invites the elegant

Berlin woman with fine, almost white hair to his house in the Vallée de Chevreuse. She meets Colombe's mother, she understands that it is 'complicated'. She gives Colombe an ecru-and-pink flowered chiffon scarf. Colombe keeps it for a long time, until it vanishes, like so many other things, without her realising, one day it was simply gone.

1989

—Really? You remember? exclaims Colombe.

—Yes, you told me all about it.

—Oh, it was nothing, just a bit of meningitis.

Colombe dares not admit to Héloïse that when they were eleven she had lied to her, she had never had meningitis but she wanted her to think she had to impress her, because she admired her.

1990

From September to June, Colombe's father is in the hospital, she goes to see him every day.

She is absolutely sure that her father is not going to die. Her mother does not tell her what the doctors are saying. She tells her vague and reassuring things.

One day he is allowed to leave the hospital to spend the day at the house in the Vallée de Chevreuse with his family. Colombe doesn't realise he is saying goodbye to her.

1992

Her mother does not say it, that he has died, but it is over.

Colombe does not see her father's body.

After the funeral, Héloïse is worried, why doesn't Colombe seem sad, why doesn't she cry?

Colombe explains to her that she can still think about him and talk to him, he answers her, so why be sad?

She is sure this is just a bad patch, that her father will come back.

She doesn't tell people that her father has died. It is possible that she is ashamed of it. She is not herself anymore.

They go on holiday to Héloïse's parents' house in Saint-Tropez. Héloïse's father goes shopping and wants to buy Colombe a present, but Colombe no longer wants things.

1992

Their degrees from good universities, their CVs, their internships at blue chip companies obtained through their parents or their parents' friends, their future careers, their ambitions.

Héloïse and Colombe have no doubt they are equal to any boy their own age. Héloïse is hired by the marketing department of a big cosmetics brand. She can't believe it when a boy who graduated from a less prestigious university tells her his salary: he is earning 15 per cent more than she is.

Colombe gets a job as a reporter on a television programme. A cameraman tells her his father is a postman. Colombe laughs; it's the first time she has met a postman's son. This laugh is one of her greatest embarrassments, one of her biggest regrets. She would like to erase it.

1992

Colombe is in love with an Englishman who is fourteen years older than her. One day, his back to her and looking at his feet, he declares he's in love with her. Another day they are standing in the aisle on a packed number 83 bus, stuck in a traffic jam at Sèvres-Babylone, he says to her, let's stay friends. Colombe turns towards the window so he can't see she is crying, she spots Héloïse weaving her way across the road through the traffic, she wishes she could climb out of the window of the bus and cling to her friend.

1992 to 2007

Colombe and Héloïse see less and less of each other.

They are busy with their careers, getting married, having children, working.

They negotiate mortgage loans and, with help from their families, find nice apartments in good neighbourhoods, near the Luxembourg Gardens for Héloïse (who receives a larger parental contribution), in Montmartre for Colombe, they both have an eat-in kitchen, a bedroom for each child, their bathroom floors are covered in zellige tiles picked up on a long weekend in Marrakech, their wedding dresses are stored in protective slipcovers, their husbands read *Le Monde* and recite Mallarmé's poetry, they give birth at the Clinique de la Muette, the private maternity hospital in the 16th arrondissement, epidural, newborn cashmere cardigans from Bonpoint, reproduction antique wooden cribs.

Colombe and Héloïse after their day at work, bent over the strollers, shopping bags dangling, stopping to kiss the baby, constantly checking, buying meat from the best butcher in the neighbourhood. They set the table, put on a roast, change a diaper, nothing disgusts them, their child's shit is delicious, one last kiss, one last hug, pay the cleaner, she's the one who vacuums, but they clean the bathtub and the toilet before she arrives, the dishwasher hums, they're exhausted, at last their husbands get home, the roast is cold, *reproach*, the right shirt isn't clean, *reproach*, the baguette isn't fresh, *reproach*, the butter has a peculiar aftertaste, *reproach*, they clear the table, he has an important phone call to make, they go to bed, reject their husbands' hands on their thighs, trying to slide farther up, in the morning they struggle to get up, spill milk on the floor, they are alone, they panic, will they make it on time, they yell at the children, they are going to be late for school, who would believe it, two bourgeois women in beautiful apartments furnished with chests of drawers from the Conran Shop, so smooth, solid, silent, the drawers closing with a light click, no effort, or it's invisible, they themselves refuse to acknowledge it. They are always guilty, the child has a cold because they didn't dress it warmly enough, the child has head lice because they weren't sufficiently vigilant. Sometimes love flickers back, their husbands buy them brightly coloured tulips and gold rings, take them to Venice, book a room with a four-poster bed for their beloved wives whose breasts have shrunk, they will never leave them, they are the family, the cornerstone of everything, the mother of their children, even if they're not much fun, actually they're difficult and always tired, it doesn't mean anything if they sleep with other women, they get home late, are mostly — though not always — discreet, the desire to be caught, to smash everything, this unbearable jail, the bourgeois institution of marriage that imprisons both men and women, the same endlessly repeated conversations, the same holidays, the same material desires, a new, more expensive handbag, a new, more expensive armchair, the tedium, sometimes they don't even have time to wash their hair, their husbands talk through dinner, interrupt them when they try to speak, it is easier to keep quiet.

The imaginary sociologist, who has not yet retired, pops her head in. She is disappointed, she had hoped that Héloïse and Colombe, given their education, their degrees, their background, their friends, would have escaped their condition as women, wives, mothers. They are thirty, thirty-five, forty years old, their heads bowed, their shoulders hunched, they are silent and downtrodden. She was convinced that thanks to their social status and their money they would be freer, less blind, their husbands more modern, the system less suffocating for them, they would rebel, find a different place. It turns out that money and class don't cut it — they are wrung out by their gender.

2001

The doctor details the process very clearly. Your mother will gradually slip into a coma, she will feel no pain, I will provide palliative care. Be present, stay by her side. Ask for help. She has about six months left.

He says, don't tell her she is going to die.

Little by little, Colombe's mother, or who she used to be, is transformed; it is a drawn-out, terrible death, the agony of sensing her slow demise, without physical pain, but with endless mental distress.

The doctor has said it, her mother is dying, that is how it is, there can be no false hope, but at least there is the certainty that she will die, and that truth consoles Colombe. She has something to fix upon.

But Colombe's mother must have figured it out, though her mind is already growing confused, she repeats words and questions, she only realises too late, weeping, her mind is fading, the end is close and there is no one to say it plainly. Her eyes are closed, she has not moved for two days, she stops eating. Colombe's two-year-old son – as he has done every single time he has come to see his grandmother since she has been sick and retired to her bedroom – takes off his clothes, lies naked on his grandmother's body, puts his head on her chest, opens his arms to touch more skin. She lies still at first, letting herself be taken over by her grandson's naked body, then she lifts her right hand and folds it around the arm of her little love, because that is what this modest woman, who has never called her own children other than by their given names, calls her grandson. Watching them, Colombe realises she cannot remember her mother ever hugging or even touching her.

LATER, when Héloïse describes these months in Colombe's mother's apartment – Sylvie and Fati, who are paid to sit with the dying woman and her relatives, to tend to the sick person, to listen to Colombe, to wash the patient's body, to cook and keep the apartment clean, to be there, to open the front door, to take the visitor into the bedroom, to close the door, to peer round the door at just the right moment, to discuss the situation with the night nurse and the day nurse, to help with the paperwork, to console, to change the sheets every day, to bring hot coffee in a porcelain cup with a cookie on a matching little plate, to say, it's not your fault, you must deal with death as well as you can, and live your own life – she recalls the kindness and calm that prevailed in the large, sombre apartment.

A different friend, not Héloïse, asks Colombe how she is. Colombe sighs.

—Not very well actually.

The friend looks surprised, then says:

—Ah yes, I suppose that's because of what happened.

Colombe understands that 'what happened', too distasteful to name, is her mother's death.

2002

Colombe inherits a considerable sum of money. She is both relieved — she tells herself she will have less to worry about now
she has money in her bank account that was, until now, often
overdrawn — and uneasy. The money has fallen from above,
with no effort on her part, no work, it is her dead parents'
money, the notary explains, the fruit of two working lives. The
money is in a bank account, she cannot listen, cannot concen-
trate, after she speaks to the notary she sees her bank man-
ager, who talks to her about investments and life insurance.
She is not interested, but she does buy herself some red boots
and a matching red leather handbag. She is embarrassed, but
not enough to give the money to charity, she keeps it for herself, spends it, buys an apartment in Paris. She knows that now
she is different from her colleagues, she is an heiress, when
most of them own only the fruit of their labour.

2005

Colombe, her husband, and their two children move to the
Left Bank, to a large apartment that looks very like her parents' apartment and is in fact very near the one where she
grew up. She enrols her children in the École Alsacienne, conveniently just down the road. Colombe and Héloïse are neighbours again, and their children are at the same school, just as
their mothers once were.

Colombe is a researcher at a television station. Her boss warns her, I don't pay you to think.

Héloïse is taken on by a prestigious consulting firm. Her boss warns her, I like working with girls from good families, they are so pleasant and obedient.

2006

They turn forty, and still have no wrinkles. The guys of their age and background, with the same qualifications and experience, are paid more than they are and promoted, which they are not. They do not think this is unfair, they think it is normal. The men spend more hours in the office than they do, they have more authority, they are confident, they speak without hesitating. Héloïse and Colombe rush home every day to take care of the children. They think they are unattractive and a bit useless.

The director of a weekly news magazine asks Colombe to write a column, but he doesn't like what she sends him. Colombe perseveres, because it's those moments when she is writing with her computer on her lap when she feels best about herself. There is no one to tell her, like her boss, that it's no good, no one to tell her, like her husband, that it's not what he expects from her. She writes something about her paternal grandfather. She never knew him, her father never talked about him. She doesn't know if this something is a book or nothing. She asks her husband his opinion, he tells her it's nothing. She sends it off to a publisher anyway. She imagines that he will be indulgent because a few years earlier he had hit on her. The publisher tells her it's a book.

Colombe knows she will have to choose between her husband and writing books, she cannot have both. The book is published, it wins a prize. Héloïse goes with her to the award ceremony, they come home together, they don't talk. They are both worrying about what will happen next.

2006

Héloïse possesses astonishing courage combined with enormous naivety, which has always worried Colombe. Héloïse never lies, so she cannot imagine anyone lying to her.

Héloïse tells Colombe:

—My husband, poor love, fell asleep in the car and spent the whole night there. He works so hard, he is utterly exhausted.

COLOMBE FINDS A RECEIPT for a hotel room in Paris on the desk. She shudders, wonders why her husband spent the night in a hotel room in Paris. She is reassured by the single room supplement marked on the bill, imagining a narrow single bed in which he slept alone, she has no idea why, but then she can't know every single thing about him. She stands by him. He hasn't cheated on her, she is sure of it. Until one day it suits her to accept the truth, so she doesn't feel guilty. She takes a lover.

2007

In the same year, Colombe and Héloïse leave the husbands who did not dare leave them.

They meet other men.

The sociologist sees this as an act of rebellion and she is delighted.

2008

They start spending holidays together again.

Héloïse's parents are members of the Saint-Tropez Beach Club. They have a canvas beach hut right by the entrance.

These are the best huts, the ones for the families who have been there forever.

The house in Le Baou is no longer a problem. They own a house in the Domaine du Cap, they have been from Saint-Tropez since forever, Héloïse's grandmother bought a small village house in La Ponche in 1951, well before it became the fashion. The rule is to have moved there 'before'. You will always find people who arrived after you, you look at them kindly but really you despise them, and when you meet some who arrived before you, they annoy you.

What matters is that you are a member of the club and that your beach hut is well located.

The beach huts for tourists and recently arrived members are right at the far end of the beach.

They have had the same beach hut since 1979, when Colombe first went to stay with Héloïse. A little canvas cottage with broad amber and white stripes, two changing rooms, shelves holding hairbrushes (clean, no stray hairs), sun cream (bought this year, not encrusted old tubes with yellow cream that oozes out when you unscrew the cap), mirrors, bathing suits neatly arranged in plastic pouches, and creamy white towels with a dazzling royal blue border.

There is a deck out front, two chaise longues, two canvas chairs, a glass table laid with a tablecloth at lunchtime by waiters in jackets; club sandwich, pan bagnat, Caesar salad, ketchup, chips, mustard, Coca-Cola, 7up. The huts are pitched in a row like tents, around them people speak Italian, Russian, English, German, Arabic, French, Chinese. The view of the sea is obstructed by other canvas huts, there is much laughter, squeals of joy and frustration, card and water games. The bodies of the rich are not more beautiful than the bodies of the poor.

Colombe and Héloïse are with their children. The kids want chips and ice cream, they want rubber rings, they don't want to play cards inside the beach hut, they don't want to sit quietly, they don't want to read *Tom-Tom and Nana*, they don't want to have a rest, they don't want to be quiet for five minutes, *we can't hear each other, we can't talk.*

The club has the most beautiful swimming pool in the world, fifty metres long, filled with seawater.

Let's go.

Colombe is terrified her children will drown.

Colombe's daughter is five, she wants to learn to swim. Colombe tells her she is too young, Héloïse says not at all. She encourages her, shows her the movements for breaststroke. The little girl has a go, she really tries, swallows water, spits it out, perseveres, Héloïse always one step behind her. Colombe stands warily a little farther away. Héloïse is filled with admiration and enthusiasm, while Colombe is afraid. Long after, she can still recall Héloïse's luminous admiration that summer afternoon, the glittering water, memories so strong they detach themselves, come towards Colombe through the white-and-orange canvas of the huts, remain vivid throughout the winter.

2009

Colombe fights with a man about a speech given by the minister of the interior, Brice Hortefeux, who has proposed stripping polygamous men of their citizenship.

Things get tense.

This man takes her by the elbow, smiles at her, and says: I will tell you what you must think.

Colombe replies, no you won't.

And she can't believe how assured her voice sounds.

—No you won't.

It's the first time in a long time.

The last time she said no you won't, or no, I don't want to, was before her father's death, when she thought she was really something.

2010

Héloïse is slim and athletic, with a child's laugh; she is often surprised by how uncouth other people can be.

Héloïse and Colombe are on Héloïse's father's boat. Héloïse takes Colombe aside and whispers in her ear: praise him for that manoeuvre, it will make him very happy. Colombe is amazed that she is so attuned to her father's feelings. It would never have occurred to Colombe to worry about her own father in this way, if he had still been alive.

2011

Héloïse tells Colombe:

—My father is going to die.

After her father's funeral, Héloïse confesses to Colombe:

—When your father died, I wasn't there for you. Not enough.

—That's not true. You were there.

WITHIN THE SPACE of a few years, Héloïse gets divorced from a man she loves and respects, and her father, whom she loves and respects, dies.

Colombe encourages her to go and see a shrink.

Héloïse listens to her, but doesn't feel it helps her very much. She stops going very quickly.

Her grief doesn't prevent her from continuing to look for

love; she seduces, loves, makes love; behind it all lies the regret that won't budge, that the man she loved betrayed her, didn't love her anymore, loved another, would never again be hers.

For her future ex-husband's birthday, Héloïse looks for a present. She has a list of ideas that she shares with Colombe. The gifts on the list are sumptuous.

2013

Colombe is fired from her job, and wonders if her career is over.

Héloïse volunteers to help; she offers to ask her older cousin to meet with her, to give her advice. He knows someone who knows the CEO of the company where she works, he also knows the CEO of the company's main competitor where she might apply for a job. She offers to lend her some money.

—But how are you going to get by, Colombe, without a job, without a husband, without a family?

Colombe says don't worry, everything is fine, even though it's not true, everything is not fine, but it's even more difficult for her to admit it. She would rather change the subject.

2015

Héloïse and Colombe are walking in a forest in the Vallée de Chevreuse.

Colombe phoned Héloïse that morning, and finally confessed to her:

—I can't take it anymore, it's too hard.

Héloïse said:

—I'm on my way.

She met up with Colombe and the two went for a walk. Heather, ferns, birches, oaks.

—You can't fight the whole world, Colombe. Pick the battles that matter, and let the rest go. Take care of your children. You have to work and earn money. The rest is not important.

Colombe, who is not accustomed to obeying, obeys her.

It's the beginning of autumn and it's as easy as that.

Colombe stretches out in a clearing, spreads her arms and legs.

Héloïse sits down beside her.

Colombe feels the blood moving through her body.

She can't get over how easy it is.

All Héloïse had to say to her was:

—Let it go.

Later, Colombe will love telling Héloïse what she owes her: the right to be a little bit imperfect.

2015

Colombe has just published a book about her father. A journalist is interviewing her about it. They are in the kitchen of her apartment, a large room with brightly coloured tiles, and a white marble table from the '60s.

The journalist asks her:

—Are you from a bourgeois family?

She responds, confidently:

—No, not at all. I am the granddaughter of immigrants.

The journalist is insistent:

—We do tend to think that the bourgeoisie is always other people. It's so undesirable, to be bourgeois. We can always point to someone who is more bourgeois than we are.

The journalist is right. She's bourgeois.

2015

Héloïse has dinner with Colombe and her children. She is in the kitchen, agitated; she has to send an email, she's waiting for another. She's glued to her phone, she has a job in the public relations department of a pharmaceutical laboratory, an underling is trying to take her job, a woman with deep cleavage and some nerve, who flatters the CEO, stole her report and put her own name to it, it's just not okay, is it, to do something like that? Should I say something? Do you think I should quit?

Her presentations, her files, her analyses, her recommendations, her PowerPoints are always perfect, and still she is always disappointed. Or, more precisely, she always feels as if others are disappointed in her.

Of Colombe's friends, Héloïse is the most serious. She isn't funny but she laughs a lot, she has a job that Colombe doesn't understand, somewhere between marketing and PR, public relations and consultancy, although she is shy, reserved, and has no self-confidence.

When she talks, describing the strategies of companies she

regularly leaves for the vaguest of reasons, Colombe pretends to listen and to approve. She admires Héloïse for a different reason.

Since she was fifteen, Héloïse has dressed like a grande dame, in her grandmother's designer jackets. She's not sexy, no miniskirts, no cleavage, just a young woman whose style is to dress like a middle-aged lady. The jewelry she wears is too shiny and heavy, she wears make-up, does her hair, wears stockings, and yet, in spite of all these violations of fashionable lefty Parisian taste, Héloïse has had, since her divorce, a string of lovers whom she leaves with the same regularity as her jobs.

She describes the reasons for these break-ups to Colombe, who listens, intently. She wants the men to be more flamboyant, cultured, funny. Or she points out they're not as brilliant as her ex-husband, or her father. Colombe tries to slow her down, reminding her of how lucky she is to have found someone who loves her. It is in these relationships that Héloïse, in her well-behaved buttoned-up silk blouses and her skirts that are never too short, fully exercises her freedom, while Colombe, in her gauzy unbuttoned cotton shirts, is more corseted.

Colombe says to her friend, but what do you really want to do, you can choose, you can do anything, you're intelligent, you have excellent credentials (thinking that she is like herself, wanting to decide, choose, direct everything), but Héloïse doesn't choose, she lets herself be led by her seriousness, her good education, her credentials, little ads on LinkedIn, her doubts; she is hired for jobs for which she is overqualified and underpaid, and the text message from her supervisor arrives and it isn't the response she'd hoped for, they're not going to give her the interesting project, instead it's going to the girl with *some nerve.*

Finally Héloïse sits down, asks Colombe's children some questions, very precise questions, smokes a cigarette, suggests to Colombe's elder son who wants to get into Sciences Po that he have a look at her own son's dossier, he has just got in on the first try, as she herself had.

The next day, Héloïse telephones Colombe:

—Do you feel sick to your stomach?

—Um, no.

—Because I feel sick to my stomach.

—Maybe you have a bug? You think it was last night's dinner?

—I've had it for three weeks. Do you think it's normal to have a stomach bug for three weeks?

—Um, I don't know. Maybe. Maybe it's normal.

2015

Colombe comes out of Franprix, it is seven o'clock, a seven o'clock in November that is exactly the way you'd think it would be, damp, brown, tiring. Her bag is full of a boring dinner, chicken breast, rice. Héloïse calls her and she answers, because whenever they speak they might be eleven or they might be forty-nine, it's nice to turn back time. Héloïse speaks in a clear voice, direct, crystalline, amazed, her usual voice, maybe the speed is a little faster, and more tense.

—It's everywhere.

—What's everywhere?

—The disease.

Colombe says yes, but the information hasn't penetrated her brain, a barrier has gone up around the word *disease*, it crumbles before it can reach the place that processes language. There is a word, *symptom*, combined with others, *gland, blood, fatal, lung*, but her brain cannot establish any links between them. Colombe hangs up as if normal life were going on as usual. The woman for whom death does not exist takes the metro, puts down her bag of groceries on the kitchen table, and then, as she is putting the chocolate yoghurt away in the fridge, she makes the connection, she is overwhelmed with nausea, she wants to telephone Héloïse but that endless stomach flu Héloïse has been complaining about for weeks has taken hold of her. Colombe is afraid, but she doesn't have a choice, she calls Héloïse, and asks the question to which she already knows the answer, which confirms everything she doesn't want to know.

—What is it you have? Is it serious?

Héloïse says again:

—Yes, it's everywhere.

COLOMBE WALKS TO HÉLOÏSE'S HOUSE, they live on opposite sides of the Luxembourg Gardens, Colombe near Port-Royal, Héloïse at Vavin.

Since they were eleven years old, everything has been equal between them, the advantages of one compensated by the problems of the other and inversely, but there, on the Boulevard du Montparnasse between Vavin and Port-Royal, there is no longer any possible comparison, or resemblance, or advance or delay, there is only – Colombe thinks, enraged – betrayal.

How can you face down death when it's standing right there, without artifice, with no means of escaping it?

HÉLOÏSE OPENS THE DOOR, they don't kiss hello, they never do, they just stand there.

Héloïse speaks first:

—I'm not afraid of dying.

—I'm going to fight.

—Till the end.

—But meanwhile I'm going to live.

—I want to travel.

—There are so many countries I've never seen.

—That's that.

HER OLDER, handsome cousin arrives, they're going to speak to the children together, tell them their mother is sick.

Colombe slips out, relieved to leave this task to him.

THERE IS NORMAL LIFE, when we don't know anything, we can't predict what's going to happen, everything is constantly modifying, changing, Stevie Wonder's 'Summer Soft' comes on the radio, a song that always takes you somewhere else, to a lost love, the metro is late, a colleague calls you to complain about something you've done, you are irritated at being misunderstood, you have an itchy rash on your neck, you have nothing to soothe it with, normal life, as it is, full of distress and relief, the passage from one thing to the next, a pendulum that will, in the final instance, freeze mid-path, certainty is a trick, death is everywhere, tearing up everything, only death exists.

So it's over, it all stops here. It's still too early. And all around us these people who live for such a long time – why not us?

They are not quite fifty years old, whatever grey hairs have appeared are barely visible, thanks to their excellent and subtle dye jobs, their smooth skin an indication of their impeccable lifestyle, their light wrinkles a sign of their reasonable bedtimes, their legs are waxed smooth, their breasts small and therefore less likely to hide a tumour; they dine on leeks, fresh salmon, and kiwi fruit, they drink one glass of red wine a day just as their doctors advise them to, and they are going to die young?

They are good girls. They go to bed early, do their homework, don't pierce their ears, don't have to repeat a year of university, don't cause concern; they smoked a joint once and it made them cough. They got married, had children, a job, they still go to bed early, they are tired, their husbands aren't around, their children are small, then they get older, it's easier, they get divorced, they have affairs.

Héloïse's illness can't be explained by any of her past choices. It is not the result of a trauma, a heartbreak, a serious wound, of overindulging in alcohol or cigarettes. When the illness comes she is happy, in love, her children are doing well, she has a job, she isn't worried about money. She has had her share of grief. She has lost her father, and her husband. This kind of grief, the kind that comes over the course of a life, measurable grief, is not the kind that can bring on a fatal disease. Otherwise we'd all be sick.

She is the opposite of a *risk case*. She is gentle and serious; she has no self-confidence. That's not a reason to contract a fatal disease.

One day, Héloïse is worried because she feels nauseous, and has for the past three weeks (but Héloïse is always worried for no reason, Colombe thinks, judging her, as if this isn't the case for her as well).

Two weeks later, her doctor informs her it's in her liver, her bones, and her lungs, that there is no treatment, it's inoperable, Héloïse is *floored*, and the clichéd language is accurate, and as for Colombe, she *can't get over it*, and the clichéd language is right for her as well. No one can say *with the life she led*, or *that's what smoking will do to you*. With the life she'd led, she should have lived to a hundred and twenty. It's not fair, we won't give in to it, Colombe protests, but she is wrong, it's not her illness, it's not her death.

Unlike Colombe, Héloïse is not preoccupied with fairness.

Héloïse knows there is no reason, no explanation: misfortune, or fate, just *is*.

2016

During the first month after Héloïse's announcement, death refuses to give an inch and they refuse as well, they exaggerate the smallest bit of positive news, transforming it as necessary. They listen and retain the figures that suit them, that create the story they want to hear. They build their own mythology, *she's going to get through this*, holding on to and repeating whatever facts allow them to prove it, no matter how thin, vague or unsubstantial. The other bits of information, with the audacity to suggest something other than what they want to hear, they don't matter, they reject them, they call them thin, vague, unsubstantial, although they are on the contrary immense, certain, powerful.

Héloïse has no chance of getting through this.

AND AGAIN THE WHEEL TURNS.

You are right to believe it, you are right to hold on to these tiny stones which you alone can interpret. You are right to be crazy and naive, to read a favourable future in these inconsistent signs. You are neither crazy nor naive. But it's not a question of luck. It takes so little to shift from one state to another, from illness and death to life, from tragedy to joy, from stupidity to greatness of spirit.

The first miracle was that her illness responded to a new treatment. That's what Héloïse told Colombe over the phone. Pills, with ridiculous side effects, dry skin, hair in weird places. They were right to be unreasonable.

Héloïse repeats these magnificent words, *the cells are dead stars.*

Can we please return to a normal life without death.

Love.

Héloïse has a new lover who has the good fortune of having the same first name as her first husband whom she still secretly loves, and of resembling her older cousin who is very handsome and very generous.

From January until the end of the summer, Héloïse and Colombe gush over this new lover, who came into her life just two weeks before the news came of this fatal illness, and who didn't run off in its wake.

Colombe also has a new lover.

2016

Héloïse's boyfriend rents a boat, she smokes a few cigarettes. Her thin, muscled body dives into the Mediterranean. Her eyes shining, Héloïse tells Colombe that no man has ever been like that with her before, he watches her for hours, he takes her in his arms, he stays like that without getting tired of it.

Héloïse is very happy.

When she comes home from her holiday, Héloïse coughs, the first treatment is no longer working as well, her doctor recommends she try a second-generation treatment.

HÉLOÏSE IS LOOKING FOR WORK, finds something, calls Colombe to describe her new responsibilities, parking issues, colleagues. Colombe puts the phone on speaker, washes her hands, dries them, catches herself in time to formulate a reasonable response.

They speak on the phone, as they always have, as they did before (when no one was thinking about death).

THEN THINGS DON'T go quite as well.

The therapies are no longer working for Héloïse.

DEATH RETURNS TO HER LIFE, but the doctors don't use the phrase *fatal illness*, they use this strange language you constantly have to translate, they talk about *critical condition, therapeutic impasse, lethality.*

The word *death* has never been pronounced, referenced, expressed, interrogated; it has disappeared from all conversations as if it were an unknown word, whereas for her, death has never been so present.

There is no one whom Héloïse can ask questions like:

Does it hurt to die?

Do you have to talk to death, negotiate with death?

How do you prepare to die?

What do you do when death is there and you have to say goodbye to life?

2017

They meet in front of the Hôpital Cochin where Héloïse will begin the first phase of a new treatment.

Colombe volunteered to go with her to the hospital; it's the only way to get out of her own head. The night before, her boyfriend had broken up with her. He kept telling her to *stop crying*, although he had spent the previous months telling her she was *the one*. Colombe wants to die, but then she's ashamed of thinking such a thing.

There's a late June heat wave, and Colombe is waiting for Héloïse, who is running late. They haven't seen each other in ten days. She sees a very pregnant woman covered in black fabric from head to toe, accompanied by a man wearing shorts who holds a small child by the hand. Then she sees another figure, skinny and hunched, whom she doesn't at first recognise, the woman looks quite old. It's Héloïse, she's having problems with her legs, her femur has been impacted, but she came on foot, she lives too close to the hospital, she hadn't dared take a taxi. Héloïse leans on Colombe's arm and they walk slowly to the treatment centre. There, they find something resembling cool air, a functioning elevator; a nurse greets them kindly and settles Héloïse in a large armchair covered in almond-green plastic, beside a window overlooking a tree. Colombe leaves while the nurse inserts the IV, she sits in a dining room / waiting room / cafeteria where there is a microwave, an ATM, the smell of chocolate, and four Formica tables. A poster offers information and advice for managing treatment. Colombe inhales slowly through her nose and exhales through her mouth, the way she's been taught to do in this kind of situation. A woman in a white blouse asks if she's there for a treatment, if she's waiting her turn.

Colombe returns to Héloïse, and concentrates on her friend's face, the end of her nose is pointier, the contour of her chin has hardened, can she do anything for her?

Yes, and it helps Colombe to help her.

Héloïse forgot the charger for her phone and is going crazy. Colombe suggests she go and get it for her. Colombe finds herself outside, at first happy to escape from the treatment she doesn't have to undergo, but outside it isn't actually better. It's too hot, and the two sadnesses are getting confused so Colombe can no longer tell one from the other: Héloïse's illness, and the gap left behind by a love that disappeared over the course of a telephone call. She walks too quickly, has to call Héloïse first because she can't remember the code to her building and then a second time when she can't figure out how to open the door to her apartment. Héloïse tells her which key to use. It's the first time Colombe has been alone in her friend's home.

She looks at the photos framed in silver standing on a chest of drawers.

Héloïse's husband in a top hat the day of their wedding, her dress made of faille, nipped in at the waist, so pretty that they'd taken her picture for a Bon Marché advertisement.

Two children in ski masks, one blue, one red, the masks devouring their foreheads and cheeks.

One of Héloïse and Colombe, where they are twenty years old and wearing bathing suits, lying next to one another on a beach.

In her bedroom, next to Héloïse's bed, Colombe looks for the charger where Héloïse told her it would be. She picks up piles of books and a gold necklace, tries to assess its value. It's the one Héloïse is wearing in the photo of them in bathing suits, a heavy gold chain that stands out against her slender body, she wonders who will inherit it when Héloïse dies, she can't find the charger.

In her bathroom, next to the sink, are luxury face creams. Colombe buys her own at the pharmacy. She studies the names of the brands etched in gold letters, reads the descriptions of elixirs, serums with prodigious powers, she opens a tube of pink lipstick, not much chance the charger's going to turn up at the bottom of a jar of Dior cream, but she can't help herself, she plunges her sticky finger into the pearly white cream, spreads it under her eyes, where a wrinkle has appeared. The charger is there beside the sink, on the white marble counter. She hesitates before opening the closet to look at the cashmere sweaters, the Chanel jackets Héloïse inherited from her grandmother, there they still hang. As Colombe puts out her hand to touch the golden threads of a cardigan, she hears someone come in. She puts the lid back on the jar of cream, closes the closet door. It's Héloïse's younger son. Colombe explains why she is in his mother's bathroom and runs out, into the street again with its oven-like heat, past the sign reading *Oncology*, into the elevator. Héloïse thanks her, she needs to be alone now, she wants to call her boyfriend. Colombe envies her, she will come back to pick her up in two hours, while she waits she will go and swim in the pool in the Rue de Pontoise, the one she used to go to with her ex-boyfriend, she sobs loudly during one of her lengths then she pulls herself together.

2017

Tests.

Héloïse lists for Colombe the succession of test scans without complaining.

She is waiting for a test or she's just had a test. These *befores* and *afters* succeed each other with regularity. Before there is always some suspense. Will things be better? Will there be fewer markers? Is the treatment working?

Together Héloïse and Colombe imagine the good news. Each time they tell themselves a story: the markers of the illness will be smaller, it will be easier to treat now. They become very excited about what might be working. *Is Héloïse pretending to believe their stories to reassure me?* wonders Colombe.

Héloïse tells Colombe what her doctor tells her: even though the treatments have failed one after another, she is still not in a *therapeutic impasse.*

And then, very quickly, the wait returns for the next test, and with it, hope returns as well.

2017

Colombe asks her: how are you doing? Héloïse responds: not well.

Still, she's doing everything right. She's eating vegetables, exercising a bit, resting, avoiding sudden emotional changes (as if such a thing were possible), conscientiously taking her medicine, drinking mineral water, attending treatments, one after the other.

She doesn't believe in alternative therapies (Reiki, naturopathy, osteopathy, garlic, green tea, lemon and all manner of prayer). She has never been in a state of denial about what's happening to her.

She is sensible, rational, obedient, and desperate, all at once; she takes up odd and extravagant new projects, I want to be an interior decorator, open an art gallery, move, break up with my boyfriend, go to India with my boyfriend, sometimes she smokes a cigarette without hiding it.

Her doctor explains to her that she must learn to live with her illness. She obeys.

2017

Héloïse states the facts, lists them, as if they hardly bothered her at all, how she fainted during a treatment, how she couldn't get up one morning, how she's afraid to be alone at home, the tests, one after the other, the ebbs and flows of the illness. She is in prison, her release is forever postponed, and we are her jailers, those of us who let her believe she might eventually get out, although her cell keeps getting smaller, every day the windows shrink, imperceptible to the naked eye, but if you don't see her for a week you can see the damage, her breath is ever shorter, her gait more awkward, and so our lies become ever shoddier and more shameful.

In precise, medical, technical terms, she talks about her illness, the treatments, the names of the drugs, their side effects; like a good little sick girl, she learns the language of the hospital, one that Colombe refuses to absorb, with words full of *x*s and *y*s, of *mo*s, of *chi*s, of *gly*s. Héloïse knows the history of all the drugs, their evolutions, the latest breakthroughs in France, in the US, the most cutting-edge pills, revolutionary, still being evaluated, not yet approved, tested on rats, mice, monkeys, cadavers, the protocols, the approvals, the laboratories, their funding, their researchers, nothing escapes her.

She is methodical, analytical, conscientious, organised, a perfectionist, she doesn't rebel against any of it. She analyses how to fight without raising her voice, using her good manners, never wavering, never giving up, please, which is the best doctor, department, drug, who knows how to access it, get the appointment, get the treatment, whatever it is, she can do it.

2017

Since she's been sick, Héloïse hasn't become any braver, stronger, more sensitive, she was like this before. The illness hasn't brought her anything, hasn't transformed her for the better, hasn't been redemptive, hasn't taught her anything about herself, it has only been a long and painful ordeal.

2017

Héloïse is suffering. The pains are physical and emotional. The symptoms are intense, though of varied acuteness; they are sometimes sharp, sometimes burning, sometimes dull, sometimes deep; it smarts, snips, cuts, saws, undulates, strikes, attacks; it overwhelms, spurts, dirties, strangles her bones, her lungs, her liver, her skull.

Héloïse says straightforwardly, without grimacing: it hurts. She sometimes says where: her shins, her lower back.

There is no such thing as empathy, no one can put themselves in her place or take on even a little bit of her pain.

Colombe is impotent, she can't imagine what her friend is feeling, she doesn't know what it's like. A burning or a shooting pain, a tearing from the inside, a pair of pliers, hammers incessantly hitting her legs. Colombe writes it down, her body stretched out with the computer on her thighs, nothing is hurting her, she's in good health, she's trying to find synonyms for pain, tearing, contraction, torture, ordeal, to try to zero in on something that can't be shared. She looks back through her memories, childbirth, a sprained ankle, a fall, and realises that we forget physical pain; it's emotional pain that returns again and again.

COLOMBE WATCHES HÉLOÏSE, who has cut her light brown hair very short. Where she always used to be smartly dressed, now she's stripped back to the simple, unadorned, genderless beauty of her adolescence. You can really see her big light eyes, she is very beautiful, although the pain has traced new lines on her face, her mouth sometimes tenses, she clenches her teeth, her hands part to rub some part of her body, to calm the lacerating feeling in her bones, the feeling of slicing in her liver, the burst of tightness in her lungs. Nothing escapes her, nothing can be soothed, everything feels like it's bursting, exploding.

Pain is unreachable, incomprehensible, for other people.

WHAT HÉLOÏSE IS MOST AFRAID of isn't physical suffering but of *losing her mind*, of witnessing herself – precise, attentive, organised – coming undone.

The doctor recommends a new treatment.

But which is worse for her mind: the treatment that risks clouding her clarity or the illness that will cloud that same clarity?

COLOMBE THINKS BACK to her mother in the final months of her life, how she had lost her melancholy humour, her biting (but never cynical) view of relationships, becoming duller with each day. And yet her mother had also been able to show love, the love she had always hidden – out of modesty and because of her upbringing – when she was *still all there*. Colombe remembers. Her mother wasn't any *less* herself, she was just another iteration, more tender, less wound up in her catastrophic childhood.

This summer, the doctor gives up on the final treatment. Héloïse stays in Paris, alone with her fear. She asks Colombe, how do I seem to you? Tell me if I start saying weird things, if I become crazy, if I repeat myself, if I stop understanding things.

Colombe listens to her attentively, no, I don't hear anything strange.

Héloïse is having more and more difficulty walking, but she insists on going home by herself. Colombe lets her, thinking only too late of the three flights of stairs she has to climb, in her elegant seventeenth-century building, the stairs carpeted in royal blue, the walls covered in reproductions of paintings, hunting scenes, courtly scenes. There is no elevator. She goes up one step at a time, each one a blow, the morphine makes her vomit. She is being tortured, but refuses to give in.

2018

Death does not exist. And yet she is going to die. Everyone knows it, it's a question of months.

What she reads online about her illness Héloïse keeps to herself: the chances of survival (none), the time she's got left (three months to a year), end-of-life things. Colombe does the same research online. But they do not discuss what they find.

2018

Colombe, Héloïse and her mother get together for dinner. All three of them are in that in-between state which is neither life nor death but rather a blurry moment where the end is no longer a far-away uncertainty, it has appeared with determination, blocking off what's left of Héloïse's life, circumscribing every conversation, and every gesture, with its gravity. It's the last time they will dine together, and they have to keep up the pretence, for her mother's sake, so she can keep some of her illusions intact, so she can get a few hours of sleep tonight. And when they say good night, when Héloïse is back at home, when her mother says to Colombe it's over, there's no point fighting anymore, Colombe exclaims assuredly: not at all.

HÉLOÏSE'S ROOM at the Hôpital Cochin isn't sad or ugly and it doesn't smell bad. It's a large, light room; a huge window opens onto chestnut trees and sunlight.

Héloïse mentions a friend who is supposed to visit the next day, he works in an American laboratory, there is a new treatment, new treatments are always revolutionary, it might be able to help her. Colombe nods, encourages her, does nothing to deny the myth of the revolutionary treatment.

I'll come by to see you tomorrow, Colombe says to Héloïse, and slips out.

Colombe thinks of all her failed goodbyes. The last time her father looked at her he was in an ambulance; he signalled to her from the window, it was the saddest look she'd ever seen him give, she'd responded with a big smile, as if he were only going away on holiday. Her mother's final gesture had been a squeeze of her grandson's chubby arm. We pretend we are going to see one another again, see you very soon we say, smiling, her father knew, her mother knew, Héloïse knows, but out of politeness for the living, they pretend to still be on their side.

In the Middle Ages, people feared dying suddenly, without time to prepare themselves, without being accompanied by the appropriate words and gestures, without being able to speak one last time to their loved ones, to say what they had to say; death was tamed (as the historian Philippe Ariès puts it). Dying alone, without saying goodbye, was the greatest fear. This unnamed, savage death is, today, our own.

2018

The evening Héloïse died, Colombe was walking near the Hôpital Cochin, without daring to go in. She would have liked to, but she didn't want to disturb her family. She sat on a bench on the Boulevard de Port-Royal, and waited for Héloïse's mother to call.

She called the next morning. She spoke with the same clarity as her daughter. She repeated to Colombe what Héloïse had said. She told her mother it's difficult to die, and Héloïse's mother asked the nurse to help her daughter die.

To hear one's daughter say *it's difficult to die* is a terrible thing for a mother, but Héloïse was accustomed to speaking without all the little mystifications that help us through things, that brighten up our lives so that we can continue to lead them.

2018

Our deaths are as unfair as our lives. Some are painful, long, grueling, and violent, while others are peaceful; the heart that stops suddenly in the chest of a woman sitting on a rattan chair in her garden; a man surrounded by family who has just gone to bed utters a feeble cry, and like that, it's over.

There are acceptable ages and unacceptable ones.

When Colombe complained to her uncle that a former lover who was sick with cancer was refusing to see her or answer her messages, her uncle explained that dying is a long and painful occupation that can only be accomplished alone or with someone to whom we are very close.

Colombe's uncle and his wife had shut themselves up at home, waiting for her to die. He went ten years later. The night before he went to the cinema and came home tired; he died during the night.

Héloïse died in a hospital room, with her children, her cousin, her lover, and her former husband at her side.

2018

A funeral mass is held for Héloïse, the church is full, her friends are dressed understatedly in light, neutral, elegant colours; the priest didn't know Héloïse, he says the obviously sad things we say about a woman, a mother, who has died too young. At the cemetery her son speaks, he is sweet and smiling, Colombe recalls Héloïse's accomplishments in gymnastics, everyone cries discreetly. Afterwards there is a reception at Héloïse's apartment, a waiter passes around mini croque monsieurs and mini chocolate éclairs. Colombe sees her old friends from the École Alsacienne, most either never left the neighbourhood or have returned to it, there are a few discreet laughs, people talk about Héloïse with emotion in their voices. Colombe looks at the photographs on the chest of drawers, the children in their ski masks, the two of them in their bathing suits. A woman, the only person dressed in black, watches Colombe leave before the others, she is the sociologist from their childhood. Death undoes everything, she thinks.

2018

During the final months of Héloïse's life, Colombe couldn't get over the fact that she wasn't restrained by illness, she could get up, run, nothing could stop her.

In the months that followed Héloïse's death, Colombe is completely out of it, she calls every woman she meets Héloïse, she's still doing it now, a year later, she feels her absence everywhere she goes, but she is also filled with an almost delirious desire to live that she didn't expect.

She is alive and the September sun is very bright.

Colombe goes to sleep with this thought: make me die. Who is she addressing? No idea. Who would have the power to make her die before her time, since she doesn't believe in God and isn't planning suicide? During the day she laughs, she marvels, she desires, she walks. She wakes with this incredible sensation: she's not sick, there's nothing holding her captive, what joy, and this joy, this desire to enjoy everything, to eat a pear sorbet that's far too cold, to walk in sunny streets, as full of life as she is of sadness at the death of her double, she can, without even trying, succumb to that exasperating modern injunction to make the most of what life has to offer.

COLOMBE WOULD LIKE TO TALK about Héloïse, but the dead don't interest anyone.

Colombe calls Héloïse's mother.

They meet for dinner. Her mother says everyone is very kind to me, but no one dares mention Héloïse.

2018

Colombe has arrived at an age when she knows many people who have died, every year there are more phone numbers to delete, she always waits too long, six months, a year, you never know, another myth, what if the dead person were to return, if he learned he had been erased, like that, without having been given the chance to reappear, that his closets have been gone through, his email, his possessions distributed and his clothes given away. You have to wait a little bit, Colombe believes, to be certain the person is really dead. Then comes the regret at having deleted the messages, the attempts to remember the number, to call back, the number has not yet been given to someone else, it rings in the void.

. . .

COLOMBE HAS ALSO REACHED the age when a former classmate has been made a government minister. She sees his
ageing face on the television, she would have liked to have
called Héloïse to say he's still really cute, isn't he? Who is she
going to be able to share her silly thoughts with now?

2018

Since Colombe got dumped, she's had this persistent pain that
makes her want to die, although she is in excellent health.
She doesn't know anyone who's in as good shape as she is, she
swims three kilometres a week, eats lettuce, sleeps nine hours
a night, takes naps, is never sick, has never had an operation,
not a single night in the hospital, such a waste of fitness and
good health. Héloïse would have known what to do with a
body as alive as Colombe's.

Héloïse dead in the midst of life, when there are so many
living dead, limp, repetitive, desireless lives, so Colombe forces
herself to get up and get on with it.

2019

Héloïse has been dead for a year now. Hers is the only life Colombe has been able to observe in its entirety, from its earliest
days — age eleven, the beginning of secondary school, all that
promise — to its end, at age fifty-two.

Colombe contemplates the various stages of her friend's life, the Kickers and roller skates on her feet, her excellent grades, her first nightclub, her degrees, and her future ex-husband's declaration of love, her jobs, her babies, her father's death, her divorce, her disappointment at the things that didn't work out. A life lived parallel to her own, except that one was cut short and you have to make do with memories. Colombe doesn't agree, a memory is nothing.

Colombe would nevertheless like to share her happy moments now with Héloïse, anecdotes that sketch out who she was, but she is confronted with the greyish fog of her illness and her death, in which there is only regret for what was left unfulfilled.

2019

Colombe returns to Héloïse's Instagram account. It hasn't been deleted.

She was ill; she posted images of the sea in Cancale in Brittany, of Gruissan in the Aude, of Giverny's flowered paths in Normandy, of trips with her boyfriend, of mimosas #divinesurprise, of blue skies, #blue, of Mont-Saint-Michel, of the abbaye de Fontvieille, of cypress trees, the flights of seagulls, *feeling zen* she wrote, #spring #happy. She had time to travel to Aswan, #roomwithaview #nile, and New York, #bigapple, #viewfromthesea. She also went to Venice and Minorca, #sea #beauty, the last image is the Eiffel Tower sparkling at night, and she wrote for the last time #parismonamour.

Héloïse kept her promise to live right to the end.

2019

Colombe thought for a long time that love was primary and friendship secondary. There was a hierarchy to our emotions.

For Colombe, friendship is easy, natural, effortless, durable, whereas love fails every time.

Héloïse met her when she had braces and never left her side. They saw each other often, then less often, then often again, without friction, or rupture, without reproach.

She asked nothing of her, Colombe had the right to have other friends, Héloïse wasn't jealous, there was no rivalry between them, no rules, because friendship commits and protects you without the strictures and obligations of coupledom. There are a thousand ways to be friends, whereas there are only a few ways to be in a couple. Society has a vested interest in romantic relationships, and therefore imposes a certain number of rules: you must have children, see your in-laws, live together. There are no such rules inflicted on friendship; it has been left in peace.

Colombe still hasn't found lasting love, but she is surrounded by lasting friendship, Héloïse being the oldest, one of the great witnesses to her life. Colombe understands that Héloïse's friendship has been a more faithful and abiding force in her life than most of her lovers. And if Colombe is better suited to friendship than love it's not because friendship is secondary, or less demanding, but because it is a bond without a model, without rules.

2019

Colombe has to call Héloïse, it's been a while since she's heard from her, Colombe still feels a little guilty for having dropped Héloïse when they were twenty for being so posh. Ever since it's usually been Colombe who calls Héloïse, and almost never the other way around.

And then she remembers Héloïse is dead.

Héloïse used to worry about Colombe: no salary, uneven success as a writer, an uncertain love life. How are you going to manage?

Héloïse wanted to give her money. She didn't want Colombe to get involved with this guy. Héloïse watched her with round, frightened eyes. Héloïse was sensible, put money aside, recycled, invested, sent out impeccable CVs and cover letters, went to meetings at La Défense with directors of human resources, consultants, coaches, made lists of her weaknesses, her timidity, her lack of self-confidence, her strengths, her sense of organisation, her meticulousness, how are you going to manage? she would ask Colombe again and again. Héloïse found a new job, told her the salary to the exact centime. Do you think it's enough? Could I have got more? Héloïse described the office, the boss, the project, and with the same level of detail her new boyfriend, his job, the street where he lived, his degree, the new boyfriend sitting on the couch in her apartment, watching Héloïse as if he had never seen such an exceptional woman. Héloïse looked at Colombe, concerned, as usual; she was single and she didn't really have a job. Whenever she finally did have some good news, a glimmer of something stable, which happened to her quite often, this hope, of money, of love, Colombe called Héloïse, and her friend was genuinely happy and relieved.

COLOMBE FINALLY GETS interested in Héloïse's career and reads her LinkedIn profile, it hasn't been deleted either, and it's a way of checking in with her.

MBA, Essec, luxury product management,
first LVMH cohort, 1989–1992

BA, Sciences Po, Paris

A communications professional specialising in influence and crisis management, I have built experience in regularly exposed and strongly regulated industries (pharmaceuticals, casinos, finance, utilities/energy). I have a solid foundation in social issues and corporate social responsibility combined with an ability to understand regulatory issues across a wide variety of sectors.

My background in both businesses and agencies as an executive consultant has allowed me to develop strategies for communicating and adapting to change and overseeing the operational implementation of those strategies, in order to benefit companies' reputations and the defence of their strategic interests.

Colombe is impressed; if she had been a boss, she would have made Héloïse a super-boss.

Maybe her forthrightness, her willingness to say I don't

know, her honesty, to say what can't be done, her rectitude, to say what is possible, were not what was required to *forge a career* in a capitalist enterprise.

2019

Héloïse wasn't angry about her body's betrayal or the doctors' inability to cure her; she always submitted to the rules, to what was expected of her, to morality; she did her best to face up to things, to bend to what was expected of a woman of the bourgeoisie. A good girl, a good student, a good wife, a good mother, a good employee. She never rebelled, she was unfailingly loyal to those she loved, and she was sad when things went wrong. She didn't understand, because she did everything right, because she obeyed, why wasn't she congratulated for her efforts, why hadn't she done that degree, why did the director of the master's programme award the best internships to boys whose grades were worse than her own, why did they lie to her, why was she betrayed, why didn't she get that promotion even though her boss had assured her that given her track record the job was hers, why was she reproached for her lack of ambition yet when she was ambitious and showed it, working so diligently, she was never rewarded for it, why was she humiliated? She never sought the answer anywhere but in herself. It was most certainly her own fault. It's simply not done, trying to break out of the place to which one has been assigned, that of the sweet and smiling young woman, well-educated, well-dressed, well-coiffed, always at the service of everyone else.

She remained in this role to the very end, even when she was sick: obey the doctors without defiance, trust them, follow their instructions, no matter how painful, perhaps it was only when it came to love, to the pursuit of love, that she found some margin of freedom, where she could reflect on the possibilities and the encounters that life offered her, right to the end.

COLOMBE FINDS OUT that after her divorce Héloïse had a secret lover, he was married, he came to see her in the hospital just before she died, and he went to her funeral where he spoke to no one.

2020

Colombe is not ready to deal with death again and is avoiding going to see an older friend who is sick. She knows she's going to die. The friend's husband is not leaving her a choice: she wants to say goodbye to you. Colombe looks for an excuse, can't come up with one, finds herself in a hallway of the Hôpital Bichat on the eighth floor. The husband welcomes her, opening his arms wide, takes her to the room, and lets her go in by herself. Colombe is terrified.

There is her friend, facing down death.

She is wearing an elegant pair of ironed pyjamas with blue and white stripes, she is fully made up, her lips lined in fuchsia pink, her eyelids matching her electric-blue eyes. Colombe still doesn't know what to say to someone who is about to die, so she compliments her outfit, her make-up. Her friend responds:

they're men's pyjamas from Brooks Brothers, it's a special kind of fabric that doesn't wrinkle, and the make-up is Make Up For Ever. Not bad for an outfit to die in, no?

Colombe agrees.

The friend tells her that she has planned her funeral, she would like everyone to listen to Bob Dylan and drink pink champagne, it's just too bad, she adds with a smile, that I won't be there with you. She tells her as well that she would have liked to live five more years to enjoy her husband, and his love, but what can you do. The friend asks her about her boyfriend and is indignant when Colombe says it's over and she still doesn't understand why. The friend says: enjoy your life, don't let yourself be dragged down by a man whose shoulders aren't broad enough to share your joys *and* your pains.

Colombe tells her friend that she admires her, she admires the life she's lived, her generosity, she admires that she's wearing lipstick, that she talks so straightforwardly about death, then they say goodbye and embrace each other.

Colombe leaves the room, something very important has occurred inside her.

Colombe is no longer afraid of death.

Her death is finally conceivable, but let it not arrive too quickly, let her still have a few years to love a man with broad shoulders and open arms like her friend's husband.

2020

Héloïse used to worry about Colombe. Stop brooding. Move on. Let go of what isn't working.

Colombe does the opposite, she is obsessive, she wastes time, she gets caught up in things that have happened and people she's lost, hoping they'll return, even though they're dead or gone from her life. She is slow to process grief, and then, for no reason, she can't believe her luck at the life she's been given. Colombe is more and more elated at being alive, she continues to triumph over death, she can still learn, progress, succeed.

So Colombe perseveres in writing this story, knowing that writing is no consolation, nor reading either; yet suddenly a sentence can create a slight disruption in the order of things, and it's this disruption that allows her to carry on, before it is her turn to die.

At Héloïse's funeral, the priest told her mother, her children, her boyfriend, *she is resurrected.* Colombe was angry, he's no better than the worst kind of fortune teller, maintaining your illusions, telling you that your Prince Charming and fortune are nigh, feeding you lies to make you lower your head and obey.

We'd all like it if life arranged itself in the end, with a flash of optimism, if at the end of the book the author could offer a *message of hope*, the kinds of platitudes that are meant to console as they are passed on from funeral to funeral, from grief to grief, your dead are not gone, they're simply absent; your dead are watching over you and protecting you; with those we love, there's no silence. These words are lies. The dead are dead, they do not resurrect. Colombe knows this now. What remains of our dead are blurry images, fast-burning flares, shape-changing memories, and their love which is alive in us.

SWIMMING:

A LOVE STORY

For M.

The happiness police are going to come
and arrest us if we go on this way.

—MAGGIE NELSON, *The Argonauts*

A week after we made love for the first time, he replaced the rear tyre on my bicycle. I have no idea how he managed it, since the bike was chained up and he didn't have the key. He turned up for dinner bearing a little glossy red paper gift bag and put it down on the kitchen table. Inside was a new inner tube in yellow and blue Michelin Man packaging. I put the little blue-and-yellow cardboard box with its cheerful waving figure on the mantelpiece alongside the bunch of tuberoses he had also brought. I took a picture of the arrangement, the packaging and the tuberoses, because it occurred to me that I had never been given such a thoughtful gift, and I should probably hang on to the evidence in case it all — this love, him — were to disappear.

HIS NAME WAS GABRIEL. I had never met anyone like him before. He was very tall, with broad shoulders, an athlete's body, and nimble, precise gestures. Even so, the first time we met for a drink he went to the wrong bar, showed up late, ordered a kir, then promptly knocked it over. He glanced at me, startled, and said, I'm not usually like this.

The first time I ever saw him he was twelve and I was fifteen. Our paths crossed again thirty-five years later, at the end of September.

THE FLOWERS WILTED LONG AGO, but the little box is still there on the mantelpiece, slightly tucked away so I don't get too nostalgic when I notice the Michelin Man giving me a friendly wave.

BEFORE GABRIEL, I was always disappointed by gifts. I'm ashamed now when I think of how I used to react. Ashamed to think of the face I made when the father of my children gave me a gold ring set with a glowing green precious stone. It was 2001, my mother was dying, it was ten years since my father had died, and I simply didn't want things anymore. Any gift that didn't come from them was of no interest for me. I was still expecting my father to walk through the door, his arms laden with presents. I was waiting for my mother to open her arms to me, something she had never been able to do. I no longer knew how to be loved. Then Gabriel came into my life. He scooped me up in his giant arms and held me tight, but not too tight — and I allowed myself to relax. So this was love. I had forgotten.

I'd had a succession of boyfriends, and yet I had spent more time imagining love than experiencing it. The reality terrified me.

. . .

THE FIRST TIME GABRIEL and I had dinner together, sitting across from each other, he noticed my unease, how I couldn't bear his eyes on me. He owned up to having watched a couple of videos of me online, they'd helped him understand a few things about me:

'The way you wave your hands around, push up the sleeves of your dress, smooth out an imaginary crease whenever someone addresses you or is talking about you, you only calm down once you start to speak. Are you really that afraid of uncertainty?'

I nodded and went home completely beguiled.

A week later, we met up in the Luxembourg Gardens. It was the last weekend in September. Our third date. I felt awkward. I scrabbled for things to ask him but couldn't think of a single interesting thing to say. We went to get a cup of tea at the refreshment kiosk. I insisted on paying.

We picked up our bicycles at the park gates. He noticed I had a flat tyre. He suggested we go by his apartment to pick up a pump. We walked up the stairs. Inside, I took it all in. It was a bachelor's apartment. The entryway cluttered with cardboard boxes, the bulging living room ceiling – water damage, he said – a wooden kitchen table he had painted bright blue, a sagging couch he had picked up off the street with cushions of similarly uncertain pedigree. He kept his tools in plastic bins from IKEA that doubled up as his closet.

We didn't stay long. I suggested he come up to my place 'to compare apartments'. We lived a five minute walk from each other. Mine was the kind of apartment filled with scented

candles, where every piece of furniture has been carefully selected to be camera-ready at all times, in case a representative
of the taste police from an interiors magazine were to show up
unannounced; I always wanted to get top marks. I thought I
had won, but I was wrong. Much later, I found out that Gabriel
is a true aesthete, with distinctive, unusual taste.

I had something else in mind as well. I had caught a
glimpse of his neck, the curve of his shoulder blades peeking
out of his shirt. We lay on the sofa, which was draped in a
quilted Indian fabric in shades of rusty pink and brown, and
began to talk. Our differences faded. I was no longer surprised.
It all seemed simple and obvious.

His sister called; he didn't pick up. Later he listened to the
message, her voice was husky and warm. She called him 'my
darling brother', said 'I miss you'. It was very sweet. My own
relationships with my sister and brother had been so tricky
since our parents' untimely deaths.

We went into the kitchen and ate some toast, it was all I
had. Then we went back to lie down on the sofa. After a
while – though it felt as if we were outside time – he kissed
me. We made love, first on the sofa, then in my bedroom.

We lay there naked against each other, his mouth on my
neck, I heard him murmur: it's too soon to say what I want
to say.

I didn't want to hear whatever it was he wanted to say. He
wasn't for me, we were so different, I wanted to paint his living room ceiling, buy him a new sofa, throw out the plastic
storage bins from IKEA. We had nothing in common, we
made no sense. I was far too afraid to admit otherwise.

. . .

A WEEK LATER I flew to Beirut. The day before I left, he told me, quite simply, that he was in love with me, he would be patient, would do whatever it took to make me love him back.

I kissed his whole body, but the word *love* stuck in my throat.

I asked him, we're so different, what would we even do together?

THE DAY I LEFT, he sent me a brief text message: *Do you have time to talk?*

I flew into a panic. I must have said something to disappoint him; he didn't love me anymore; he realised I wasn't good enough for him; I had too many flaws; he had seen through me; I had been too judgemental about his sofa and his bulging ceiling; he had fallen in love with someone else, a woman who was a good person, who didn't have interior design issues. Or worse: he was sick, the disease was incurable, it made no sense to be starting a relationship.

I forced myself to call him, feigning nonchalance.

He wanted to wish me a safe trip and tell me he had found something we had in common: we both owned the same brand of dishwasher.

I laughed. I was relieved: I wasn't in love with him. I was right, it made no sense for us to be together.

THE FOLLOWING EVENING, I told him via WhatsApp what I had been afraid he had been about to say: that he had changed his mind. He understood, then, that I have a tendency to let my imagination run away with itself and assume the worst.

He told me it was pointless to be constantly awaiting calamity, projecting myself into a future that is, by definition, uncertain; of course, life is sometimes filled with disappointment, just as it is with good things, but the point is there is no way of knowing.

It seemed I could say anything to him without fear of being mocked. And so I found myself fearlessly telling him I was in love with him.

ALL THROUGH OUR nine-month relationship, my fears returned to haunt me.

Sometimes I imagined him with another woman; more often, dying, injured, dead.

The last time I panicked for no reason, he was meant to be meeting me at the swimming pool. He'd warned me he was running late. I counted my lengths, ten of breaststroke, ten of crawl, and he still hadn't turned up by the time I had completed my final ten lengths of backstroke. He wasn't coming, he'd forgotten me, he'd left me, he'd had a cycling accident, he was in a coma, he was dead. I took a shower, tried to force myself to stop thinking like this, but I couldn't figure out the reason he hadn't come. In the changing room, dripping wet, I fumbled for my phone.

He'd left me several messages. *My love, I forgot my trunks! I'm waiting for you by the entrance.*

He told me he had no doubts about his love for me, he kept

telling me I was the love of his life, but he couldn't make any promises, the love between a man and a woman, unlike that for a child or a parent, was not indestructible.

He was still trying to locate the deep bond of intimacy between us.

I was going to have to get used to the uncertainty of our love.

Gabriel was a musician. A month after we met he wrote a song for me. He played it, accompanying himself on the piano. It was called 'Colombe Awakens'. He had been unreachable for the whole day, of course I panicked, had he already forgotten me?

No. He had been busy writing this song for me, and I had no idea. I was like a toddler who thinks that when you stand in front of them and cover your face with your hands, you have gone for good.

He sang it in his lilting voice, calling me 'my darling', promising me his uncomplicated love, no regrets, days of joy, no fear, forever. I was so moved listening to him that I had to lie down on the floor. I believed it and he did too, how naive we both were. Uncomplicated love does not exist.

He kept telling me: I love you truly, madly, deeply.

ONE SUNDAY IN NOVEMBER, Gabriel rented a Renault Kangoo to transport our two bicycles. He had planned everything down to the last detail. He had made a reservation for lunch at an elegant restaurant with yellow flowered curtains, the kind you find in small towns, that serve appetizers of foie gras and smoked salmon. The town was a few miles from his family's holiday home where we had first met thirty-five years before, and from my parents' holiday home, which I had not been to since they had died. It was like a little frontier town between the past – his family, his home, my family, or what's left of it, my home – and something that was taking shape between us. I showed him the news stand where my father used to buy *Le Monde* on Saturday afternoons, and the butcher's store where we went on Sunday mornings and the butcher would give me little slivers of saucisson.

Gabriel put an arm around my shoulder. As we walked, I felt the solidity of his body against mine, and that was when I made peace with my memories; or to be precise, the good memories snuffed out the bad ones, my parents' untimely deaths, my loneliness; all my fears evaporated.

The château hotel was lost in the fog. He had booked the nicest room, with a four-poster bed. He took out champagne and raspberries from his backpack.

We stayed in the room until dinner.

I took a picture of the rumpled bed after we made love. I wanted a trace, proof that it was real: the high windows looking out onto the gardens, the wooden paneling in the bathroom, the enormous bed, his body. All the sorrows of the past made sense now; this was the culmination. It was real, though I couldn't help imagining ourselves as characters in a different story.

We had met as teenagers, found each other again, fallen in love, and this time there would be a happy ending.

The following morning, we finally emerged from the hotel. He pointed out a deer standing at the edge of the forest. He told me how one morning in the Pyrenees the previous year he had gone for a run. Ahead of him he glimpsed a deer crossing his path. He saw it as a sign of hope: he was going to meet a woman he would love and who would love him back. A hundred yards ahead of us the deer stopped, looked at us calmly, then vanished into the forest.

Gabriel likes stories with happy endings too.

In the afternoon we stopped at a farm. We each bought a chicken for our children and some fresh-laid eggs. When we got home that evening, I boiled the eggs, and he made toast soldiers. I said to him: I don't need chandeliers and foie gras, I don't want to be a princess dreaming of a handsome prince, I just want to eat soft-boiled eggs with you in the kitchen on a Sunday night.

HE MADE ME a shepherd's pie after I told him it was one of my favourite dishes. He was no cook, it was not an activity he enjoyed, but he went shopping, mashed the potatoes, braised the ground meat in tomato sauce, and brought the whole thing over to my apartment. I was bowled over; but was it already too much?

He thought that love must be fought for. He indulged what he thought he discerned in me.

Much later, in a letter, he wrote that he 'was intoxicated by a dream of a world record as pointless as it is out of reach'.

He wanted to achieve perfection. I don't believe in perfection; I know my faults only too well.

HE TAUGHT ME that I have a body. Before I met him, I didn't have a body; my arms, legs, neck – they were a part of me, but of no consequence. I didn't appreciate them, I was barely aware of them, paid almost no attention to them. I held myself badly, stood hunched and lopsided. I fed it, kept it moving with a bit of physical activity, walking and cycling. He kept saying: your body is as important as your mind. I was surprised. In my family, if the body was sick, it was examined, prodded, treated. 'Does it hurt here if I press?' I'd think about it. 'Yes, a little, maybe.' 'What kind of pain? Sharp? throbbing?' I'd think about it again. 'How about your stomach, thigh, ankle, wrist?' This limb, though I barely ever noticed it, clearly existed.

It allowed me to move, stand up, sit down, feed myself, walk, run if I had to. If all that was functioning, it was good enough.

That was how I was brought up – not to inhabit one's body, not to touch it, it was shameful, quite absurd to be interested in it, it was not to be thought about unless it was damaged or painful – then it could be talked about, but not too much, because complaining was not allowed.

What about love and sex? How to deal with that if we pay no heed to our bodies? They must be reclaimed on command.

I explored Gabriel's body, stroked the pads of his fingers

and the fold behind his knee, clasped an ankle, traced the spot where his neck met the hairline, the crack between his buttocks, the corner of his lips, the inside of his cheeks, his nostrils, his armpit, the left nipple and then the right, each testicle, searching for where the skin was finest, most sensitive. I gradually learned to abandon my body to him, let him do what he wanted with it. I almost lost my fear. Sex is a game without end, there are infinite ways to be touched, caressed, penetrated. He made up new rules that I joyfully accepted. I was heading towards a new, unfamiliar destination.

Sometimes, the fear returned.

HE SUGGESTED WE GO swimming together. I walked behind him, there were stray hairs on the floor of the showers, under the harsh lighting nothing was spared, scars, cellulite, varicose veins, wrinkles, creases, curves, mottled skin. Your body may not be perfect, but it can still be revealed.

Everyone leaped into the water with the same enthusiasm. They kicked their legs, extended their arms, shared the same water and the same effort. Was I meant to belong to this group? I wasn't sure it really appealed. I watched Gabriel, his broad, muscular body, black trunks, orange towel with a picture of Snoopy, the vigour and restraint of his movements. I didn't want him to be disappointed in me, so I got in and slowly swam a length of breaststroke. I was cold, my left foot was stiff with cramp, I kicked the lane rope. I tried something that resembled the crawl but stopped, out of breath, after one length. I kept on swimming though, because he kept on swimming, because the otherbodies – older, with more scars, cellulite, grey hair, in their practical caps and goggles and-swimsuits – kept on swimming. I swam thirty lengths of gentle breaststroke. One kilometre.

My hair was wet, despite my swim cap. I had red rings around my eyes from the goggles, my skin smelled of chlorine, and my nose was shiny.

You did well, Gabriel said, but later he told me: that's not enough. The way I used my hands, the position of my neck, the extension of my back. He showed me the different strokes, he understood movement, how to hold one's hand at an angle so it splits the water without resistance, how to relax your shoulders while lifting them high out of the water, how to draw your elbow back, let it rest for a fraction of a second, how to lengthen your wrists to gain precious centimetres. He mimed the position of hands so they plunge gently into the water. I watched, tried to copy him, but I was a clumsy beginner. Patiently, he opened up an unfamiliar world to me, that of the body, a world where words are unnecessary. The one thing I knew how to do was talk. He encouraged me to look and feel. I couldn't get over it. He told me I had to improve. Strive for perfection, in everything. He told me to watch slow-motion videos of world champion Michael Phelps, his magnificent dance.

He made me see the poetic grace of the body that had, until then, been foreign to me; so many new substances, flesh, muscle, skin, bloodstream, body hair, nails, that had all been locked away and were now slowly unfurling.

Pay attention to a shoulder, an elbow, the spine, a thumb,

where to put it, how to move it, extend it, relax it, hold it straight. Feel the wrist loosen, then tense. I tried, I couldn't, he showed me again. The explanation doesn't filter through conscious thought, the movement must be repeated until it becomes part of you. I didn't know any of that yet. I had so much to learn, but it wasn't the kind of book learning I was used to; it was an unexplored, parallel world, the world of sensation. I started off as though I understood, I pretended to understand, pretending already had its effect. I corrected myself. It wasn't enough. I was still afraid, it surprised me, the knot growing in my stomach. I tried to be reasonable: there was no reason to be afraid, something had come up, he hadn't turned up like he'd promised he would, he had forgotten his phone, panic overwhelmed me, reason was useless. He'd vanished, he was dead, injured, he didn't love me anymore. There he was. He took my hand and reassured me.

WE WENT SWIMMING together again. Afterwards, we treated ourselves to a kebab, it came with sauce that dripped down my coat, that was good too.

Gabriel asked me endless questions, he wanted to know all about my past love affairs. I talked and he listened.

I told him everything, held nothing back because he wasn't judging me. Then it was his turn to talk about his life, his lovers. We seemed to have made a surprising number of similar choices, not necessarily the right ones, which amused us.

His big body, so solid, so dark, like a fortress that the tiniest thing might undo, and it would shatter.

MY FIRST LOVE, when I was five years old, was my teacher Marlène Gauneau, a tall, elegant lady with brown hair who wore a grey-and-white suit. She called me Colombine, while my beautiful mother, Hélène, always so reserved, forever locked up inside the walls of the convent where she had been hidden during the war, had never been able to give me an affectionate nickname. Madame Gauneau wrote on my report card, 'One day Colombe will forget her head,' or 'Colombe looks delicate but this is deceptive, for she is extremely determined.' She loved me despite my flaws. I simply loved her.

On the first day of school, she took us to the school library, began reading us a story, stopped after two pages, and said: when you can read by yourself, you'll find out what happens next. And so was born my boundless appetite for reading. I loved Marlène Gauneau.

THE FOLLOWING YEAR, I was smitten by Martine, the canteen supervisor with bouncy blonde curls. She would tell us about the restaurants she went to in Montparnasse.

I was fascinated by her hair and her outings to restaurants, I loved her.

I was also besotted with a little girl in my class, Christine. Everyone wanted to be her friend. She had a blonde pudding-bowl haircut and was just the right side of tubby. You wanted to give her a big hug. I was the opposite, thin and nervy, my ribs showed, I was ashamed when I put on a bathing suit. I dreamed of Christine's cuddly body.

She invited me to her house. Her mother, a nurse, had left a sex education manual for children in her bedroom.

The pictures fascinated me. Particularly the one of a man's penis penetrating a woman's vagina.

I wanted to hold Christine's hand, cling to her soft body.

WHEN I WAS TEN, Bernard Pivot invited a young American novelist who had just published a scandalous novel onto the television programme *Apostrophes*. I asked my father to buy the book for me, which he did, without suspecting anything.

It was the story of a satanic teenager raised in Hollywood who drank the blood of her mistresses. I must have read it ten times. The narrator describes the pale grey silk dress that drapes over her hips, talks about the heroine's sexual perversity, how she had been abandoned by her celebrity parents, an actress and a director. She has a lover, a producer, who is, of course, rich and handsome. She describes them making love, their positions and erotic gestures. Her boyfriend handcuffs and blindfolds her. I was captivated by it all. My father figured out, too late, that it was not appropriate reading matter for someone my age.

MADAME ALLEGRA, Christine Allegra. My classical dance teacher at the Schola Cantorum, the music and dance conservatory on Rue Saint-Jacques. She was not very tall, she wore her brown hair in a pixie cut. I didn't love her, but I admired her. I wished she would adopt me.

Between the ages of seven and thirteen, to begin with once a week, then two, three, four, five times a week, I attended Madame Allegra's dance class. She was so attentive and encouraging it blew my mind.

When I was a child, I had a body; it was only in adolescence that I forgot it. In ballet class I contorted my legs and arms, stretching and bending at the waist; my toes were bloodied from the pointe shoes; I tried to do the splits every day, but I wasn't supple enough. My mother, la belle Hélène, would wake me every morning by pinching my back; she would ask if I preferred big pinches or little pinches. She had no idea how to hug or kiss; though she loved her children desperately, she was unable to show it. The only reason to have a body was for the physical endurance and regimented violence of classical ballet.

I told my parents I would like to join the Paris Opera as a *petit rat*. My mother said nothing, but my father said, 'If you become a dancer, you must be a great dancer. If you're going to be average, it's not worth it.' Dancing is joy: the joy of unfolding your hands, thrusting your thighs into the movement of the melody, swaying your hips to the rhythm of the notes, pirouetting, moving your ankles back and forth after a silence, picking up the rhythm again as you raise your head; it is dizziness, too much music, too many movements, losing your mind, laughing, no longer knowing which is your body, the parquet, the reflection in the mirror.

ON THE ADVICE of Madame Allegra, I went to see a Russian ballet teacher at her studio at Châtelet. I took the number 38 bus on my own; I remember my panic, the nervous feeling in the pit of my stomach, the crowds of people hurrying past, I didn't manage to punch my ticket, and was horrified that I might have committed fraud.

The Russian ballet teacher examined me, observed the position of my shoulders and arms, touched my skinny legs, asked me to do the splits, which I managed but barely, knelt down to force my feet into the correct position.

She straightened up and shook her head. *Nyet.* I would never be anything but an average dancer. It was not worth my while to persevere, to let my wrists, neck, head, ankles, back,

buttocks, every finger, be used in a great deployment of sensation, to suffer minor injuries and then forget, to listen to every
note, following the music, its rise and fall, letting it float,
the movements and gestures following one after another, not
knowing which is leading — the note, the movement, or the
gesture — a single soul, united.

I was more concerned about Madame Allegra's disappointment than my own, and before long I stopped going to
her classes. If I was not going to be a great dancer I might as
well give up altogether. And so, in adolescence, I vacated my
body.

Fifteen years later, on the platform of the Sèvres-Babylone
metro, I saw Madame Allegra standing on the opposite platform. I couldn't tell her all she had given me by encouraging
me to dance, or how I had once admired her.

I WAS OBSESSED with sex and love. I wondered if I was normal.

On a weeklong horse-riding camp, I spied on a couple of
instructors. She had large, hazel eyes, he had long hair and a
red bandana knotted around his forehead. They lay on the
lawn beneath a plaid wool blanket, kissing each other on the
mouth.

I watched them. I was twelve years old, and I wondered if I
would ever be kissed, touched, loved like this young woman.

I WAS FOURTEEN, fifteen, sixteen years old; at last boys were
beginning to look at me. I liked it.

. . .

I WAS EIGHTEEN, I had two lovers who lived on the same street. One was serious-minded, the other less so. I thought having two lovers was ideal and perfectly normal, since my father did too. He had always had two wives, my mother and another, younger-looking woman. It all ended badly, of course. I was not my father, and all I was left with from this brief three-month double life was a sense of shame. I said to myself over and over: I'm so ashamed, I'm so ashamed.

I WAS TWENTY-THREE, my father died, and I became invisible to all men who were not him.

I WAS THIRTY, about to marry a man I chose because when we first met, he told me: if we ever get married, I promise I will never leave you, but I will definitely cheat on you. That seemed quite a reassuring proposal: he would be like my father, but he would never leave me as my father had by dying. My husband would be immortal.

TWO MONTHS BEFORE THE WEDDING, I met the smartest, most beautiful, funniest, most elegant woman I had ever come across. I adored her. Her name was Claire Parnet, and she was fifteen years older than me. One night, I dreamed of her. I was lying in her arms, she was wearing a grey cashmere sweater, in my dream I could smell her linden-blossom perfume. I listened over and over to Serge Reggiani singing 'The woman in my bed is no longer twenty,' thinking of her. My new husband understood that I was in love with her.

When I was in labour with my first child, my husband dozed off on a bench at the hospital. I called Claire and she rushed over and stayed with me during the birth. She is my son's godmother.

We spent our holidays together.

I told Claire my mother was dying. She didn't say anything.

Then la belle Hélène died. I called Claire. She never called me back. My husband knew how much I missed her.

Pregnant again, I stopped sleeping in the marital bed. My husband tried to console me. He often stayed out and, since I am not my mother, we decided, logically, to divorce, ten years after we were married.

AND SINCE THEN? asked Gabriel.

Brief, messy love affairs that go nowhere.

All it took was an encouraging text message or a night of passion for me to imagine it was love. I would lie alone in bed, dreaming of him hurrying over, taking me in his arms; I made up conversations that went on all night; we were in Guernsey, it was raining of course, the two of us sheltering beneath a huge tree in our matching beige raincoats, keeping one another warm – an entirely invented, magnificent romance that trickled straight out of my imagination.

Reality doesn't exist, I don't trust it, in real life I don't deserve to be loved, I'm a bad girl, never lovable enough.

. . .

A MIRACLE TOOK PLACE the year before I met Gabriel.

I realised I couldn't solve everything, be responsible for everything; I had to give up fights whose outcome I didn't even care about.

I was filled with a sense of freedom.

Lying there in bed, I felt the blood flowing through my body again, the wall collapsing. I couldn't believe it. I felt myself again.

Yes, I certainly was a bit selfish, a touch ambitious, but surely I was allowed to be a little flawed.

Out of the blue, I felt like someone who could be loved.

I AM FIFTY, five foot two, one hundred pounds, my chin is beginning to slacken, I have the odd white hair, eyes sinking ever so slightly into their sockets, dry skin. There is so much time to make up, twenty-seven years of being invisible. I walk past a café or into a store, stand in line at the airport to check my suitcase, and I can feel it − not all of them, no, most are indifferent, but it only takes a few, in fact it only takes one. Men are looking at me again. I have buttocks, thighs, shoulders, an upright bearing. I stroke the inside of my forearm from wrist to elbow, with the tips of my fingers, its softness.

A year later, I met Gabriel.

Every day he would take something out of his black nylon backpack:

—A small plastic container of pumpkin soup cooked by his mother and labelled with my name.

—Another small plastic container, identical, wrapped in shiny red paper also labelled with my name, containing short-bread she had made, he would tell me, especially for you.

—A baguette baked in the shape of a heart.

—A pot of tiny tea-coloured roses.

—A natural sponge inside which nestled a little jasmine-scented soap, for washing and massaging. The soap has long since worn away, but I have kept the little sponge to rub against my body.

Gabriel used to like to place a hand on my buttocks, caress them, slip his finger between them, he would say, I've never desired a woman as much as I desire you. He was exaggerating, but I was happy to believe it. I touch my belly, my thighs, my arms, the same body he loved to touch.

—A toasted-sandwich maker wrapped in glittery pink

paper bound with an electric cable. He said it was for my children. I took a picture of the glittery pink package for fear that one day I would have nothing but memories to cherish.

The children and I spent lots of evenings trying out all sorts of toasted sandwiches, with mustard, pickles, ham, cherry tomatoes, Reblochon, goat's cheese.

HE WOULD TURN up at my apartment and take these gifts out of his black nylon backpack with a grand gesture, put them on the kitchen table, then stand and watch me with a smile as I unwrapped the packages.

HE INVITED ME TO SPEND a weekend with him in Rome. We made love on the terrace of our hotel room, didn't go to any museums, he rented a red scooter, I sat behind him and let him drive me around. We found ourselves wandering around a park, decided to make up a story, a story to terrify us.

An infatuated couple go to Rome for the weekend, leaving their teenage daughter behind in Paris; when they return, she has vanished. Her disappearance exposes the secrets and lies they have managed to conceal from each other so they could be together.

I was so caught up in the story we were inventing that I forgot we were in a park, forgot to be afraid.

I used to be scared of stories with unhappy endings, but now I was with him I wasn't scared anymore. They were only stories.

. . .

WE PLAYED happy families.

HE HAD A key to my apartment. When he came in, he would call out, 'Hey honey, it's me, are the kids in bed already?'

TO MAKE ME LAUGH, he appended my first name to his last name.

WE PLAYED TENNIS with his daughter and my son, bought ham and cheese baguettes, ate chocolate éclairs, lay on the grass.

I WAS HAVING A CONSTRUCTIVE conversation with my daughter about her uneven report card. At the end of the conversation she said, 'Want to know something weird, Mom? You're a way better mother since you've been with Gabriel.'

HIS YOUNGER DAUGHTER told me: if you write a song, you can be part of the family. I wrote a song and sent it to him.

WE HAD LUNCH with his mother every Sunday. I felt like I was part of a family.

. . .

ONCE WE WERE having supper in his kitchen with his daughter. He made up a game where we each had to try to lob a plastic bottle into the trash can. It was silly fun.

ONE DAY, I needed to cut an extra key for the front door, so I asked him for his. He handed it to me as if it were red hot. After I had made the copy, he refused to take it back. We stopped playing happy families.

I WAS LISTENING to Elvis Presley's 'Jailhouse Rock', he pulled me up to dance, I let myself be led.

He's very tall, I'm very short, and it was no effort for me to be physically in harmony with him.

I didn't want to see how he bent, contorted himself, to adapt to my height. What was perfectly easy for me was not so easy for him. He concealed his effort with such elegance I wasn't aware of it. Somehow all the tiny things he did when we were together were invisible to me. His supple movements as he leaned down and twirled me around as we danced. In the water, doing the crawl, as his arm emerged from the water he seemed barely to move, he looked so slow, yet with a single stroke he covered a great distance; he had this polite way of making everything look easy, nothing must ever weigh on other people. I am the opposite: little, tense, clumsy.

. . .

HE TOOK A TRIP to Montreal with his younger daughter. They planned a surprise for his elder daughter, who was living there. She had no idea her father and sister were coming to visit. He was going to disguise himself as a delivery man, with a beard, baseball cap, and glasses, and hide his younger daughter in a big cardboard box, and then he was going to knock on the door of her dorm room. I was entranced at the thought of his daughter's delight.

He sent me photos of the delivery. He had hidden his phone in his breast pocket and filmed the whole thing.

His elder daughter knew immediately it was him. The younger daughter burst out of the box and they all fell into an embrace.

I was in Paris, on my own. I thought it was quite wonderful. I wanted to tell the three of them how hugely I admired them giving each other such love.

WHEN I THINK back to the gifts I gave him, I realise they were primarily intended for me. They were designed to turn Gabriel into the man I wanted him to be.

—A white shirt from A.P.C. so he would look like all the men in our neighbourhood, with their careful designer stubble.

—A deodorant from Aesop, an Australian brand designed to identify the wearer as an international Bobo. It was to re-

.   .   .

place his usual one from Franprix, which I found a bit nonde-
script.

To PLEASE ME, he went out like this, in his white shirt, smell-
ing of Aesop, but it wasn't him.

HE SENT ME a text message when he got back from Montreal:
*I've been having dark thoughts about our relationship. We don't
have anything in common.* I rushed over to his apartment, slid
into bed beside him. He was cold, I warmed him up. Up until
now, it had always been the other way round, it had always
been he who warmed me up.

I told him this story of Ernst Lubitsch.

—Do you know the difference between a Jewish romantic
comedy and a Christian romantic comedy?

—No.

—In a Christian romantic comedy, the enemy that keeps
the couple from being together is external. They are physically separated, by the ocean for example, or a prison wall, or
society, or their parents forbid them from being together. The
lovers must fight this enemy, go through trials and tribulations, and prove how brave and fearless they are so that they can
be together. In a Jewish romantic comedy, the enemy is within.
The heart of the person who loves and is loved is trapped in a
carapace of fear, jealousy, torment. The lovers may fight, go

through trials and tribulations to try to smash this carapace, but it will all be for nothing. The enemy within can only be vanquished by itself.

We had to talk.

Gabriel said, I can't love you like your father did, with that kind of love.

He was right, and that was the night, twenty-five years and ten months after his death, when I finally broke up with my father. My father was not the perfect man. This was the most precious gift Gabriel gave me.

THE NEXT MORNING, he took out from his suitcase a pair of gold earrings shaped like tiny anchors ('to match that preppy coat of yours' he liked to tease me about), and three jars containing Canadian honey, samphire salt, and camomile flowers.

I cried, thinking how sweet the gifts were, and of the night we had just spent together.

I asked him if his dark thoughts would return.

Yes, he warned, they might, maybe in six months, maybe never.

We were so different.

I tried to reassure myself with thoughts of the tiny gold anchors and the pot of honey, two sticky gifts. But my fears were back.

BEFORE, he had been just an outline. A twelve-year-old boy with dark hair, standing at the edge of a swimming pool. The picture, taken in spring 1981, is slightly out of focus. I was fifteen, he was the son of my mother's new friend Anna, a sculptor with long, gleaming brown hair. She was very beautiful.

MY MOTHER AND ANNA met at a parents' evening where they both offered to accompany the class on a school trip to Rome. The parents were told the schedule for the trip, and the rules, and when the teacher said they would be sharing a hotel room Hélène's anxiety shot through the roof.

How could she possibly share her room with a stranger? She would have to undress in front of her, conceal from her who she really was, that is to say a Jewish woman in a constant state of anxiety. When this woman found out Hélène was Jewish, she would be bound to regard her with suspicion. Hélène would have to show herself in her underwear (they had been told there were no private bathrooms in the hotel) and then she would have to try to fall asleep next to a likely anti-Semite. It would be better not to go. Hélène didn't belong in that world anyway. When she was with other mothers from school — most of whose pupils were the offspring of either the well-to-do upper middle classes, or eminent intellectuals from the Parisian bourgeoisie — she always felt invisible, exiled from the group. She sat there, ensconced in her anxiety that one day no doubt she would laugh about once she realised how absurd it was. And then she glanced round and met the bright eyes of a woman who seemed to be smiling at her. She smiled back. Both women raised their hands at the same moment and, even though they had never exchanged a word, said with one voice that they would be happy to share a room. Somehow they knew they would have a lot in common.

HER NAME WAS ANNA. Of course she was Jewish, with an Italian father and a mother from an old French Jewish family. She had been in New York during the war, and her anxiety levels seemed slightly less extreme than Hélène's. When Hélène got back from the school trip to Rome, she declared triumphantly, I've made a new friend.

With a fifteen-year-old's naive arrogance, I looked at my mother's new friend and her twelve-year-old son, and I thought, well, it *is* possible to be Jewish without fear, without exile, without destruction.

Just as I was wrong about the unconventional, painful, deep bond of love that held my parents together, I was wrong about this too.

In June, Anna invited us to spend a day at their house in the country. There we were, my mother and I, in our summer dresses, ready to leave, when in walked my father.

I was hoping that, thanks to Anna, my mother was finally going to unshackle herself from him, leave him, meet another man, a faithful man, and be happy at last. But my mother loved my father, my father loved my mother, he always came back to her, and neither of them wanted to split up and be alone. I was fifteen, and convinced I knew better than both my mother and my father about what they should do with their love, it would be better for them to separate.

Hélène announced our plans to her husband, my father; we were going to spend the day out in the countryside with her new friend, Anna; excellent, he said cheerfully, I shall come too.

Hélène was delighted but I was furious. He always ruined everything, he didn't want her to have a life, to spend time away from him, and as usual she messed everything up by agreeing.

She should have refused, got on with her new life without him. But she didn't want a life without him, it didn't interest her.

Anna and Hélène 'lost touch'.

And the twelve-year-old boy?

Thirty-five years later we were to meet again.

The first time we saw each other after all those years was something of a missed opportunity.

We were standing at the school gates. It wasn't the morning rush, the jostle of children and parents greeting each other, but the press of parents who either didn't work or worked from home, had lunch with their children, and brought them back to school at two o'clock.

It was the school we had both been to, for we had not managed to escape the allure of the corridors of privilege.

He smiled and introduced himself. He didn't look anything like the twelve-year-old boy I had last seen. He had heard about me occasionally from his mother, who had read one of my books. We had a brief, banal conversation. He'd been married and divorced, had two children, still lived in the same neighbourhood. I nodded. Me too. He smiled again, said goodbye. He didn't suggest meeting up. He didn't ask for my number.

SOMETIME AFTERWARDS, lovers by then, we were telling each other about our lives, our missed opportunities. He admitted that when we had met that day outside school, he had said to himself: if I were to get together with Colombe it would be serious, and since I'm planning on sleeping around, I am not even going to flirt with her. It was as simple as that: newly divorced, he wanted to sleep with lots of women.

THROUGHOUT THOSE LONG post-divorce years, I oscillated between the conviction that I was irresistible to every man I met, and the conviction that I was invisible to every man I met. Gabriel's indifference proved the latter. But then, in a burst of confidence in my irresistibility, I decided that (a) he was shy, (b) I intimidated him, and (c) since we hung around the same school, neighbourhood, social circle, we were bound to run into each other again.

Actually, no.

In all my affairs that year, indeed in every affair I'd had since my father had died twenty-five years earlier, I was the girl who remembered how much her father had adored her, and who could not but believe that the same undying love was lodged, somewhere, in the heart of every man who got close to her. That girl tumbled from a great height every time.

I beat the record of the most dumped girl in the world; in France; in Paris; in my neighbourhood.

PERHAPS THE LESS confident men who tried to get close to me might have loved me with complete devotion. I fled from them, they kept trying, but it was impossible, there was a wall keeping me apart from love.

So much for supermarket psychology.

MEANWHILE, we were living three hundred metres from each other, our children went to the same school, the one we had gone to, we had friends in common, and yet our paths never crossed.

TWO YEARS AFTER our underwhelming encounter at the gate of our children's elementary school, in what turned out to be an acceleration of our soon-to-be affair, we bumped into each other at a cinema.

I had been invited by the producer of a documentary I was directing to a showing of a movie for which he had composed and performed the soundtrack.

I was there with a friend. It occurred to me it might be worth trying a different approach – the application of the principle of triangular desire. Gabriel would develop an interest in me precisely because I was desired by someone else. It might have an interesting outcome. I stuck close to my friend, as if he were my lover. I greeted Gabriel, who barely responded, and went and sat in another row next to the friend-playing-

. . .

the-role-of-my-lover. I can't even remember his name now, but I do remember my disappointment.

This time, I was sure he found me too old, too unattractive; he was far too good for me.

THREE YEARS LATER, as we lay in bed together, he told me he had watched as I walked towards my seat, daunted and disappointed to see me with someone else, and he hadn't taken his eyes off me as I sat down next to my friend.

AFTER THIS BOTCHED ENCOUNTER, I carried on piling up more rotten relationships.

My friends, worried about my attempt to break the record for the most dumped girl in the world, tried to counsel me on how to improve my score in the other direction.

You have to make yourself desirable, you have to be capricious, absent, mysterious, unresponsive; you must make him jealous, you must never call, and you must always wait twenty-four hours before responding to a text. But because until my father died I was the most spoiled, capricious, insouciant, unfaithful young woman ever, I had exhausted my rights, and now I had to be available, obedient, convincing, faithful, patient, kind — and show evidence of it.

I occasionally played according to the rules, displaying the requisite disinterest, but it was tiring. For three years, I was in love with a man who loved me back for the sole reason that I managed to elude him. I held back, feigned indifference, quite the talented actress. Oh, I forgot, so sorry, I was busy. He always came running. It made him afraid. He was very much in love. He sang me love songs in Italian, called me every hour, begged me to take time to see him, confessed his fears. I was as fearful as he was. I would have died rather than admit it to him.

One day I made the mistake of confessing that I loved him and, since he loved me, we could be happy and free together. That didn't interest him, he said. Later, he admitted that he did everything he could to make people dependent on him and then once they were, he tired of them. At that point I do everything to get rid of them, he said. Which is what happened to me in the end.

There were other men. It was never any better.

The man on Tinder posing with his red car, glass of champagne or bottle of beer in hand, wearing sunglasses, showing off some part of his body, torso, stomach, shoulders, ass. At the beach, in the mountains, on a leather sofa, at a desk, in front of his beloved truck, looking straight ahead, to the side, down at the ground; snapping a picture in front of the mirror with his phone; with his children, his wife, his dog, his cat. His name is Karim, Laurent, Jean-Pierre, Cédric, Giovanni, he quotes Lao-tzu (often), declares himself the kind of man who likes to Seize the Day (very often) or Live Life to the Fullest! Or Life is Beautiful!!! with a lot of exclamation marks. He is six foot tall (he apologises for citing this detail, but he's been told it's important). He describes himself as generous, caring, athletic, divorced, a father, married, working in education, IT, social policy, marketing.

THERE ARE THOUSANDS OF THEM, all looking for love, so many of them, lyrical, boring, caring, swearing they adore going to the opera at Bayreuth. They are on Tinder.

We look at each other. It's always disappointing. I know in advance nothing will come of it, but I go anyway. And the moment we first lay eyes on each other, I hope I'm going to be wrong, I've put on make-up, a nice outfit — it was worth it, you see, you always think it's over before it's started, you didn't want to go, you were wrong.

I think of the heroine of Doris Lessing's *The Golden Notebook*, a single woman who can't help seeing in any man who speaks to her, however unattractive, as the man of her dreams. This one has a nick on his chin from a hurried shave before our date, his aftershave is too strong, he's ready to fall in love in a second, everything he says about himself turns out to be untrue. I go home feeling soiled, appalled by his lies.

His eyes are hidden behind his sunglasses. We look at each other. Might this be the one? He talks about himself, I listen. I try to imagine us together. Occasionally he asks me something, I answer. I want to show myself as I am, to be loved with all my flaws: I'm a little bit selfish, slightly aloof, impulsive, ambitious, stressed, worn out. He interrupts me, I hear how he talks about his ex, she's an idiot, his current relationship, it doesn't mean anything. And I notice all of a sudden how he doesn't look at the waiter when he takes our order, the scratchy acrylic of his beige scarf, his tiny little professional, social, financial boasts: I make deals, it's like a game of chess, I know what's-his-name, I'm going on holiday to Saint Barth, to Courchevel, the Doge's Palace in Venice, have you been?

I'm in Vienna, a museum city, cast in aspic, for a few days. In the cafés they serve matzo ball soup like my grandmother's. I go to the Secession Building and stand in front of Gustav Klimt's *Beethoven Frieze*. In the last section, which illustrates Schiller's poem 'Ode to Joy' and is titled 'This Kiss to the Whole World', a colossal man lies on top of a woman. I look at the naked man, his broad shoulders, muscular legs, expansive back, the woman's slender arms wrapped around his neck. A huge man and a petite woman swathed in a golden halo, their bodies melting into each other, their faces burrowing into their arms, their feet wrapped in blue filaments. They are enclosed within a sheltering, gilded dome, surrounded by men and women, white-faced, eyes closed, respecting their intimacy, they are all alone in the world, and I think: this, this is what love looks like – nothing like anything I have ever experienced, I have only ever loved neurotic, skinny intellectuals – a strong man with broad shoulders and a slender woman, swathed in a golden halo.

The museum catalogue gives a brief history of the frieze: 'It was acquired in 1903 by a collector, who removed it from the wall in seven pieces. In 1973, the Republic of Austria purchased the valuable work, restored it, and in 1986, it was put back on display.'

What an excellent summary of Austria's amnesia regarding its Nazi past. In fact, after it was exhibited in 1903, the frieze was purchased by one of Klimt's patrons, Carl Reininghaus, who sold it to another of the painter's champions, the wealthy industrialist and collector August Lederer. In 1938, the Nazis stole it from Lederer's Jewish widow, Serena. After the war, the work was returned to the Lederers' son Erich on condition it was not taken out of Austria. Erich, who lived in Geneva, eventually agreed to sell the painting to the Austrian state in 1973.

SIX MONTHS after my return from Vienna I met Gabriel, and realised he was the broad-shouldered man from 'Ode to Joy'.

At night, he tore off his clothes, leaving his underpants and socks still tangled in his jeans on the bedroom floor, and got into bed naked to wait for me. I did the same, so I could curl up against him as quickly as I could. My pretext was that I was always slightly cold. His body was always warm.

We were molten bodies swathed in Klimt's golden halo.

There was a red sheepskin rug on Gabriel's bedroom floor that he had picked up at a consignment store. Its deep polyester pile muffled the sound of his footsteps for his downstairs neighbours, and it was pleasant to stand on in bare feet.

On my bedroom floor there was a kilim in muted shades of pink, almond, grey, brown and dusky blue. I had picked it out with great care. It was rough on bare feet, not thick enough to muffle the sound of footsteps.

He was a man without pretension, all that mattered was love, his big bed on the red rug, his warm skin against mine, the gentle, firm way he had of wrapping me in his arms that made me feel both protected and free.

It was the happiest love I have ever known in my whole life, nine months of love that began thirty-five years ago. It was so right, so familiar, that even now we are no longer together, even though he has repeatedly told me our love makes no sense, it is as if I am still in that red room, wrapped in those arms whose girth, muscle density, skin colour I can still detail with absolute accuracy, can still feel the ease and abandon of his movements.

I could go through all the evidence of our love affair, the memories, the photographs, the trips, the flowers, the declarations, knowing that none of that matters. The only truth was our bodies, clasping each other in a murmur of meaningless words. Love is naked truth. It has no material concerns, no decorative beauty.

HE COMPOSED ONE LAST SONG for me called 'Mano a Mano', he sang, *My Colombe is lying there half naked, at a loss for words.* Which is exactly how it was.

One sultry summer evening, he told me our love made no sense, we would never be able to build anything together. We came from different worlds, he said. I lay down naked on the kitchen floor and waited for the pain to go away.

The song he had written for me three weeks before it ended, 'It may not seem so, but I have you tight in my arms', and even now I sometimes still cling to those words.

SIX MONTHS BEFORE WE MET, I wrote a short story. A man left the woman he was in love with. He hid himself in her handbag and followed her everywhere without her knowing it.

It was my fault he had left me. I had predicted it. Next time I'll be more careful, I'll write a love story with a happy ending.

It had been two months since we had split up. We met for dinner at the Italian restaurant we often went to when we were together. We shared a dessert, a frothy sabayon that the waiter kept pouring into the bowl until it spilled over onto the saucer. The first time we ate there I had made up my eyes, he told me I was beautiful, I was thrilled he thought so. He snapped a picture of me with his phone but it came out blurred.

This time I made up my eyes again, a spritz of the perfume he liked, prepared a little speech about love.

He told me again what he had already told me, and I gave him the answer I had already given him.

—Our relationship has no future. We're too different.

—That's why it works so well.

At that very moment, a man stopped by our table and reminded me we had been at school together. He took my hand and touched it with a gesture of surprising intimacy.

—Every single man seems to be in love with you.

—Are you jealous?

—No, on the contrary, it's time for you to meet someone else.

—I don't want to. Maybe it's you, maybe you're craving a passionate affair. That's what you're missing when you're with me.

—I don't want a passionate affair, I was madly in love with you. Don't you remember when I climbed over the railings outside your apartment in the middle of the night because I had to see you?

Of course I remembered. He didn't have the code for the gate, and he didn't want to wake me, so he climbed the two metre metal spiked railings that protect the entrance from the street, ripping his jacket on one of the spikes.

SIX MONTHS BEFORE he had loved me to bits, but now that love was gone.

Where was it? What had become of the love that had made him nearly impale himself on the railings outside my building in the middle of the night?

Love isn't a gold bar, he said. It's born, it lives, changes, dies. But unlike us, it can come back to life.

THE NEXT DAY, I watched François Truffaut's *The Woman Next Door* again.

The film is narrated by a woman in her fifties, Madame Jouve, who recounts the tale of a love affair between Bernard, played by Gérard Depardieu, and Mathilde, played by Fanny Ardant. When they meet again, ten years after their relationship ended, Bernard is happily married to a glowing young woman called Arlette, they have a little boy, they are blissfully in love. When they hear that someone is moving into the house next door it saddens them, for it means they will no longer be able to make love in the garden. Their new neighbour, it turns out, is Mathilde, Bernard's former lover. She has married an older man. Thanks to him, she is recovering from the years of depression that followed her break-up with Bernard.

Mathilde would like to see Bernard again. He does his best to avoid her, but inevitably their paths cross and they begin an affair.

Their affair can never be happy. Bernard is still in love with her and is prepared to leave everything behind for her. She accuses him of being cruel and unpredictable. They stop seeing each other but their separation, like their love, is impossible. He becomes violent. She is hospitalised for depression. '*Ni avec toi, ni sans moi*,' Mathilde tells him. Neither with you, nor without me.

The narrator, Madame Jouve, tells how twenty years earlier, she too had tried to commit suicide after her lover left her. She threw herself from a fourth-floor window onto a glass roof that broke her fall. She has been disabled ever since. She receives a telegram from the man she had once been so in love with, saying he would like to see her again, but she cannot bear him to see her old and in pain. '*Ni avec toi, ni sans moi*,' she declares.

While Mathilde is in the hospital, Bernard tries to go back to his happy marriage. His wife is pregnant. But Madame Jouve encourages him to visit Mathilde, who is desperate to see him.

He agrees.

They make love, Mathilde kills first him and then herself. Their bodies are discovered entwined in each other's arms.

I loved this film so much as a teenager, but when I watched it again I was angry with Fanny Ardant's character, the way she destroys the man she loves, and with Madame Jouve, who refuses to see the man she was once so in love with, and drives Bernard towards destruction and death. I have since found out that the young actress who played Arlette died two years after the film was shot, burned alive with her husband in a car crash at the entrance to the tunnel to Saint-Germain-en-Laye. Her name was Michèle Baumgartner. She was thirty-one.

I loathe this '*Ni avec toi, ni sans moi*,' I loathe love that is not joyful, I loathe Madame Jouve.

I was in heaven, and I knew it. I looked at myself, I looked at the two of us, Gabriel and me, and I had no doubt that this was heaven.

I asked him if he agreed. Well, he clarified, because he was more scientifically minded, we are in a state of completeness.

At the beginning of our affair, I asked him what kinds of things we might do together. We're so different, he said, I guess we could go to Franprix together. We lived so near each other we both shopped at the same supermarket.

We did go to Franprix, but more often he would suggest I join him on Saturday morning at the market on Boulevard de Port-Royal where my mother used to buy her groceries, and which had always seemed to me a reflection of her, bleak and depressing.

We picked out enormous mangoes, corn-fed chickens, pale, crisp romaine, lamb's lettuce, oranges that he would juice later for his daughters and me, it was festive, the market on the Boulevard de Port-Royal was a magical place.

He placed me on a pedestal, anticipated my slightest wish.

I kept asking him, what about you, what do you want? He wanted nothing.

He was content with what he had.

He didn't want to own things, but if I insisted, he would say: a grand piano, a room where I can play at night without disturbing anyone, in a house in the middle of nowhere. I approved. I wanted to go there with him.

We could not have been more different. My phone was always ringing, friends, dinners, parties, drinks, lunches, stories, reminiscences, shared histories. He warned me, I am free every night, I haven't been invited out to dinner for two years. This suited me very well. Since he agreed to everything, I forced him to join me for dinner with my friends, he was always extremely bored.

He suggested I observe what was going on; listen to the way everyone talked about themselves and showed so little interest in anyone else; watch as they grew febrile and restless, wanting to draw attention to themselves, seeking praise, interrupting each other all the time.

I kept quiet and listened. He was right.

I only wanted to be with him, I never knew where he was going to lead me, I couldn't guess what he was going to say, what his thoughts and ideas would be.

And yet I couldn't help it, I wanted to flaunt him, look, he is a god of the dance, he towers above you all, how magnificent he is, I have been waiting for him all my life – admire him! I overdid it, it was so easy, he never said no.

He was upset, this was not his life, he never wanted to go

back there. He began sleeping badly, and then one morning in early summer he woke up very early, stopped smiling, and left.

Three days later, he came over for supper. It was very hot. Loving each other is not enough, he told me, we don't make sense together, we're never going to be able to build anything. We've been living in each other's pockets, we've learned a lot, it's been interesting, it's woken us up, sharpened our senses – but we will never be able to build a life together.

I lay down naked, spread-eagle, on the kitchen floor, begging a god I do not believe in that it wasn't true, it wasn't going to stop, we weren't going to go back to the way things were before we met.

Before you, he once confided in me, I was a bit depressed, I had resigned myself to living without love. I told him, I was a bit depressed too, I had also resigned myself to living without love.

He was so tall, I was so short, he owned three pairs of jeans, five T-shirts, two black sweaters, one down jacket, one coat, I owned thirty pairs of pumps, sandals, and boots, dozens of dresses and sweaters – and yet when we were in each other's arms, our legs tangled, and we kissed, we were as one.

It was paradise, and then it was lost.

Since then, I haven't dared go to the Port-Royal market. A Carrefour City mini-market has opened down my street.

He gave me a pair of noise-reducing headphones to listen to music and shut out ambient noise. He'd asked me what I'd like for my birthday. I told him I liked tiny ear studs. He couldn't find any he thought were pretty enough. He decided that some excellent-quality headphones for listening to music was also something to do with ears.

The headphones introduced me to a part of myself I had never known, listening, which he correctly guessed I needed to develop. I had listened to lots of music with cheap earbuds.

A few years ago, I asked a famous novelist: would you rather enjoy an idyllic love affair and write a bad book or experience an unhappy love affair and write a good book? She answered without hesitation: experience an unhappy love affair and write a good book. Without a doubt, I would choose the first option. I would much rather he came back to me and this book was no good.

He composed two songs for me that celebrated our life together.

Were they bad songs because he was singing about happiness?

Is happiness in love worth nothing?

It was poetry that spoke to me in the end. *How much sadness for a silly little song? How much remorse to pay off a thrill? How many tears for a melody on a guitar? There is no such thing as happy love.*

THREE DAYS AFTER we broke up, I put on the headphones and listened to Marissa Nadler's cover of Leonard Cohen's 'Famous Blue Raincoat'. Her voice cracks, but she is present. She sings Cohen's heartache, 'And you treated my woman to a flake of your life'. The man in the blue raincoat stole his wife then abandoned her. Yet he misses his friend. 'I guess that I miss you. I guess I forgive you.' I listen to another Marissa Nadler song, 'We Are Coming Back'. Her voice is softer, she is taking no risks. I admire the beauty, there is something enchanting, almost bewitching. It is a song of happiness, and her voice is less vibrant.

I had convinced myself that all that had happened before we met, all the obstacles, suffering, joys, lessons, break-up, rapture, liberation, had inexorably led me to this place where we were together. We were destined for each other.

Our break-up shattered my naive belief that our lives have meaning, that a kind of logical construct had led me to him and him to me.

Life is not a story, it has no meaning, it is only a succession of coincidences, misfortunes, and luck.

I was the girl who always wanted to control everything, who was afraid of everything that did not bend to her will, and now I was no longer in control, I was bewildered, I couldn't understand the point of our break-up, but perhaps there was no point.

I didn't know what to do, so I went swimming. It was the only thing that offered me a succession of logical actions, one after the other: find a swimsuit, swim cap, goggles, towel, stuff it all in a bag, get on my bicycle, pedal, find a free changing room, undress, put on my swimsuit, pull on the cap and goggles to keep the water out, slip into the water, and swim thirty lengths without thinking, take refuge in the repetition.

I had a mission to carry out, one kilometre.

To begin with, I swam in a frenzy, as fast as I could. I was out of breath, I had to stop, I had forgotten what Gabriel had shown me.

I focused on my movements, one arm rising effortlessly out of the water, an outstretched hand diving down and drawing the water back beneath the body, taking in a gulp of air, head tilted to one side half under the water, mouth only partially open so as not to breathe the water in, expelling the air underwater, holding in just a little, extending the body beneath the surface of the water, marking time with the beat of my legs.

Ten lengths of crawl, when I used to not be able to do more than one.

I was filled with euphoria as the water caressed my arms, belly, thighs; as I lay on the water, I was with him, part of his world.

I began to dream about him all the time.

WE ARE WALKING in the mountains, he leaves me in front of a huge ice wall, I dare not go on without him. Snow is piling up.

When I wake in the morning, the mattress is warm and dry. There is no avalanche for me to face alone. I call him, tell him about my dream, he says, you see, we are apart, but that doesn't prevent us from loving each other.

ANOTHER DREAM: we are in the same room. He is in love with another woman.

I tell him, this time, you will love her forever. He says: if it didn't work out with you, it won't work out with anyone else. I am adamant, *you're wrong*, but I hope he is telling the truth.

My eyes close, I feel his arms around me; among dozens of others I always know it is him.

. . .

HE HAS COME to find me. He leans down, he is so tall, I am so short, and he kisses me, his tongue in my mouth, the place it occupied so easily when we were together. Our bodies press against each other, once again we are as one.

SOMETIMES WE ARE WALKING side by side, I stop to make sure he is still there with me, he stops too and beckons me to him, puts his arms around me.

WE MEET UP and make love.

HE IS GONE by the time I wake up.

It was four months since we had separated. I was sitting in a café on my own, there was a couple sitting at the next table. They were both elderly, they must have been together forever, she mentioned an apartment they had lived in in 1991. She talked very loudly about her fatigue, her cancer, she was even more tired than she had been when she had been having chemo, she reproached him for having forgotten to buy batteries for the radio she listened to every morning when she was in the bath. He stood up to go and get some from the Franprix down the street. It was still open at 8 p.m. She said again how idiotic it was, he had to be less absent-minded. He walked out of the café, she carried on saying in a loud voice, what an idiot, what an idiot, she repeated it several times. She had cropped white hair, a beautiful face, lively eyes. He was back already. He was tall, smiling, he wore a jacket and a tie and still had a full head of hair. Instead of thanking him for the batteries, she reproached him again for his absent-mindedness. And then they started talking about something else. She reminded him how he had, when he was a politician, often crossed paths with a well-known journalist. He played it down, oh, I only bumped into her once, outside the pharmacy. She insisted, no, she called you for an interview. Ah! Yes, you're right, I forgot. It's lucky for you I'm still around, she said.

I stopped listening and went back to my book.

Then she was off again, she seemed to be telling him off, I didn't know what it was about this time but I heard her say, you're a real pain in the ass, you get all worked up for nothing, just be quiet, it's intolerable. He was trying to defend himself, no, not at all, I'm extremely even-tempered. He tried to laugh it off as if it were a joke. To no avail. She went on and on.

He ended up turning away from her so as not to have to listen to her anymore. The waiter brought their order. He turned back to face her. They fell silent and drank their coffee.

I felt sorry for him.

At another table, a man was waiting for someone. He ordered for two. When his companion arrived she sat down without greeting him.

Gabriel was kindness itself, I could not begin to enumerate his attentive gestures during our nine months together. It was extraordinary. I tried to emulate him but didn't always manage, I'd forget he was there, or not ask his opinion before deciding something that concerned us both, I'd be going too fast, gently he would hold me back. I knew he was disappointed in me. I said to him, I don't know if I'll ever be able to live up to your expectations. Pull up a chair, he said, laughing.

When we were together, he called me my love, my sweet, my little Schnecken, my darling, my open book, my dove; he always went on ahead to hold open the door for me, he carried my bag, told me I was beautiful and sexy, he climbed over the railings outside my apartment in the middle of the night, he bought my kids a toasted sandwich maker and thanks to him I scored a lot of points, sometimes he got goose bumps when I kissed him, he wrote songs for me — and yet I knew all that happiness couldn't last. I had read Joyce Maynard's account of the tragic end of her relationship, gasping with horror. Even while we were still together, I was already mourning our separation.

WHEN JOYCE MAYNARD was fifty-eight, after twenty years of being on her own, of solo travel and disappointing relationships, she met Jim on the internet.

They made love in a hotel room in Budapest, after a ten-course meal. Jim, who spoke little and took a lot of pictures, snapped the moment, there was a mirror above their bed. Two people who were not so very young, who had eaten too much, who were happy. I think about this photo often, even though I have never seen it.

One evening in December we were lying in each other's arms after making love, I told Gabriel I had never been so happy in my life and he said, we should take a picture of this moment, then he said, actually we don't need to, we'll always remember it.

Joyce Maynard and Jim were as different from each other as Gabriel and I; she rushed headlong into things, he was very patient; she was used to doing whatever she felt like without asking anyone's opinion; he took up a lot of space; she liked to get away, to escape, and then come home again.

They had their routine, they ate out or at home, went on bike rides, saw their adult children. The relationship was not always easy, but they made it work.

They were happy enough, a couple much like any other. Their life was pleasant, a touch monotonous. There was no story.

Then one morning Jim's urine was orange, and by the afternoon the future they had dreamed of was over. He had pancreatic cancer. Maynard writes about how she learned, because of his illness, what it was to love someone. No more compromises or negotiations about the other person's desires, tastes, or habits; during the two years they had left together they shared everything. *Our heart was one.* After Jim died she found a small notebook in which he had noted down every day they had spent apart when she was away.

During their three years together, they had spent 118 days apart.

.   .   .

SOMETIMES, cycling in Paris, I would fantasise about getting into a terrible accident and falling into a coma; Gabriel
would come to my rescue, and we would finally live together,
like Joyce and Jim, with one heart.

Whenever he told me he was dreaming of true harmony,
what he meant was that I had not understood what love is, when
the heart and body are as one. When this miracle occurs, there
is no more doubt, yearning, squabbling. There is no more story.
True happiness in love means sharing daily life, emptying the
dishwasher, shopping at Franprix, farting in bed, wordless
glances, there is nothing to write about.

It was five months since we had broken up. We met by chance at the local pool. I was having my obligatory pre-swim shower and there he was. He had already swum. We greeted each other briefly.

The next day I went back to the pool, I was doing the crawl when I saw him pulling on his swim cap and goggles.

He watched me swim, told me I still had a problem with my elbow and forearm. I pushed off for another length. He was watching me closely: your elbow is better, but your hand is slowing you down, it's ready to plunge back into the water, but then it comes up, fingers in the air, at the last moment you're drawing back.

THERE IS SOMETHING almost spiritual about the way the body moves, you only have to observe a gesture to decipher the associated emotion. There I was, thrashing about furiously, fighting, then at the last moment I managed to check my pace, embarrassed at my ambition. The hand must dive straight down into the water. Gabriel showed me.

He said, are you okay with this? I'm not bothering you?

I laughed and gestured towards the showers to indicate that I was about to get out.

When I came out of the changing cubicle, dressed but barefoot, he was waiting for me.

We stood outside in the cold and shared a ham baguette, he didn't have time to sit down and eat. We kept on our helmets and fluorescent yellow anoraks. He was in a hurry to leave, I told him, again, that I didn't want to be friends.

He smiled indulgently and said, we know what we were yesterday – lovers – and what we are today – friends – but as for tomorrow, we have no idea.

He remarked on my new bicycle lights, the kind that attach with stretchy little bands and recharge like a phone. It felt like he was looking for a pretext to prolong this moment with me, but I must have been mistaken.

A week later, I called him. I was perfectly aware that you must never call a man who has left you. My friends were always telling me: 'You must never call a man who's left you.' We talked for two hours. He meant to tell me he'd been thinking about something, he got mixed up and said, I'm always thinking about you. When I called him out on this slip of the tongue, he denied it, I never said that.

It was six months since we had split up. He came for dinner at my apartment. I made spaghetti alle vongole because he'd once told me that one of his favourite memories of us was linked to eating it together one evening, after I had been to a funeral and he had been to watch his daughter playing volley-ball. I had riffed on the classic recipe, added tomatoes, onions, basil. I asked him why he loved me, he said, because you're pretty, actually I think you're beautiful, because I adore making love to you, because you make me delicious things to eat. It was simple.

This time I was careful, I stuck to the classic recipe, no to-mato or onion. A clove of garlic in olive oil, a pinch of dried chili, half a glass of white wine.

I sat and waited for him. I didn't know what was going to happen. I didn't know if he was going to turn up, what time he would arrive, if he would draw a bunch of flowers out of his backpack, if he would call out, it's me, like when he had the key and used to come in without knocking, I didn't know if we would make love, or if when he arrived he would kiss me on the cheek as he had taken to doing, I flinched every time, I couldn't bear it. I was still afraid.

The last time we'd had dinner together in my kitchen it was a hot summer's night, I didn't know anything then either, I thought we were together for life, and then he announced that our love made no sense.

That was six months ago.

He hadn't changed out of the blue shirt he'd been working in all day, he'd cycled from the other side of Paris, his hair was all over the place. He was very handsome. He gave me a post-card with a picture of a sailing boat.

He asked me about the men I was seeing, who was flirting with me, who I liked. I didn't want to tell him anything, but I did mention a violinist. He made a disgusted face and mimed positioning a violin under his chin.

OVER OUR SPAGHETTI ALLE VONGOLE, I eventually admitted that I couldn't help but see signs in our encounters at the pool. We were still in love with each other.

He said no, you're imagining associations that aren't there, there's no point thinking there's anything between us anymore. What are you hoping to find by chasing these illusions?

I GREW ANGRY, hissed at him, go away, I don't want to see you anymore.

.   .   .

I LOWERED MY EYES so as not to see him leave.

LOVE IS A LAND of savages.

A month later, I was invited to take part in an event at a local bookshop.

I spotted him, half hidden to one side. He left before the end.

But perhaps I confused him for someone else.

I FOUND MYSELF revisiting the time we spent together, like a series of episodes I was going to write about in sequence as they happened. I wanted to identify a romantic mythology in our love affair that I could modify according to the desired outcome, leaving out whatever did not unfold in the way I wanted, lying by omission as I conveniently forgot drab little details, casting us in roles that we had not always played. I forgot that there were two of us, and that he was not around anymore.

The cruel truth is that there is no explanation.

And yet the only function of telling this story is to flush out a tolerable conclusion to console me for what no longer exists except in my dreams.

It's been a year since we broke up. Now I swim three times a week.

To avoid running into him, I began going to different pools.

I have tried out all the pools in Paris, Nantes, Le Havre, Bordeaux, Marseille, Rennes.

I could write an encyclopaedia of swimming pools.

The architecture of the 1930s, with its high, cracked windows, the curvilinear tubs of the 1980s, the massive cruise liners of the twenty-first century that bear you far away. Fifty metres is swimming in the sea, anything less than twenty-five metres is swimming in a box.

The luxury of the individual cubicle where you can leave all your things; the shared changing rooms where you have to store everything in a plastic locker, in winter there is never enough room, everything comes out crumpled.

Communal showers where swimmers eye each other up as the hot water pours down their bodies.

The water temperature: at 75 degrees it takes a couple of lengths to find it pleasant, at 82 degrees just a few strokes.

I have been taking lessons. I love it. Fanny and Aurélie taught me to extend my body, to reduce unnecessary movements and so reserve my strength for when I need it.

I learned to plunge my hand and twist it slightly so it splits the water, becomes a support to help me float so I can let myself be carried forward by the momentum. I learned to push off, extend my hand effortlessly, draw my arm back towards me, glide forward with a slight kick. Thirty lengths. It's almost easy.

WHEN I AM not in the water, the air, its sharp wintry bite or its summery languor, reminds me of last year, when we were together.

WHEN YOU DO THE CRAWL, the shoulder comes forward with the arm extended as far as possible, the hand stays loose – the principle is to make no unnecessary effort; when the arm is in the air it isn't helping you move forward, it's at rest, refuelling, ready to move when it is back in the water, when it will propel the body forward. I am learning the principle of letting go.

THERE WAS ONE DAY when I went farther.

A PRECISE MOMENT when, with a slight push of the legs, I felt my body break free, another push, and another, my head underwater, breathing out very lightly at the same rhythm, I didn't need to take in air, I was amphibious, four, five, six, seven, eight, nine times my hands plunged into the water, my face looking down towards the blue floor of the pool, I didn't need to come up for air, it was superfluous, there was nothing keeping me on solid ground. I was completely inhabiting my body, it was an entirely unfamiliar freedom, bodily freedom, rapture, a sensuality that I alone was responsible for, all I needed was a current of water that matched the temperature of my skin, becoming one with it, transporting me, weightless, into a limitless realm.

Whenever I so much as mention Gabriel, my friends gently advise me to let matters take their course – it's the era of *letting go* – which I find impossible, life is too much of a struggle. But there, in the pool's liquid embrace, I need only an imperceptible flicker of my thighs, an arm reaching effortlessly into the air, towards the other shore, and I am borne on its infinite waters.

At last I can feel it. My fear has gone.

I am no longer afraid that Gabriel will die (because he is alive), that he will get sick (because he is healthy), that he will leave me (because he has already left me), that he will no longer love me (because he no longer loves me), that I will never fall in love again (because before I fell in love with him I had no idea that I was going to fall in love with him). I am no longer afraid that my children will die, I am no longer afraid that I will be discarded, I am no longer afraid that people will think I am pathetic, or not very nice, I am no longer afraid of getting a brain tumour or missing my train, I am no longer afraid of not knowing what the future holds, I am no longer afraid of reality. I am here.

I am no longer afraid of the waning of a man's love, because it always wanes.

SWIMMING HAS TAUGHT me uncertainty.

And with that, love returned.

Acknowledgements

I wrote these three novellas because I had no choice, not thinking they could be published; if they are today, it's because these women were more perspicacious then me, Annie Ernaux, Juliette Joste, Lauren Elkin, Natasha Lehrer, Pamela Druckerman and Susanna Lea.

I would like to thank Olivier Nora, Heidi Warneke, Christophe Bataille, Myriam Salama, and Alina Gurdiel (Grasset); Manuel Carcassonne, Alice d'Andigné, Paloma Grossi, and Vanessa Retureau (Stock); Mark Kessler (Susanna Lea Associates); Virginia Smith, Caroline Sydney, and Katie Hurley (Penguin Press); my friends who read and reread the manuscripts, Sophie Avon, Pauline Baer de Perignon, Laurence de Cambronne, Natalie David-Weill, Hélène Devynck, Stéphanie Dupays, Florence Hussenot-Houdouin, Anne Heilbronn, Laurence Heilbronn, Emmanuelle Lepic, Alexander Maksik, Laurence Marchand, Claude Moureau-Bondy, Priscille d'Orgeval, Yael Pachet, and Monica Sabolo.

Salomé Hurtado and Balthazar Hurtado, thank you for your patience with your mother.

In memoriam

Gilbert Schneck, Hélène Pachet Schneck, Emmanuelle Prat Flobert, Pierre Pachet, Jean Marc Roberts.

Bibliography

Annie Ernaux. *Les Armoires vides*. Paris: Éditions Gallimard, 1974.

Annie Ernaux. *Cleaned Out*. Translated by Carol Sanders. Champaign, IL: Dalkey Archive Press, 1996.

Annie Ernaux. *L'Événement*. Paris: Éditions Gallimard, 2000.

Annie Ernaux. *Happening*. Translated by Tanya Leslie. New York: Seven Stories Press, 2001.

Simone Veil. *Les hommes aussi s'en souviennent. Une loi pour l'histoire*. Paris: Éditions Stock, 2004.

Pierre Pachet. *Sans amour*. Paris: Éditions Denoël, 2011.

About the Translators

LAUREN ELKIN is the author of several books, including *Art Monsters: Unruly Bodies in Feminist Art* and *Flâneuse: Women Walk the City in Paris, New York, Tokyo, Venice, and London*, a BBC Radio 4 Book of the Week, a *New York Times* Notable Book of 2017, and a finalist for the PEN/Diamonstein-Spielvogel Award for the Art of the Essay. Her essays on art, literature, and culture have appeared in the *London Review of Books*, *The New York Times*, *Granta*, *Harper's*, *Le Monde*, *Les Inrockuptibles*, and *Frieze*, among other publications. She is also an award-winning translator, most recently of Simone de Beauvoir's previously unpublished novel *The Inseparables*. After twenty years in Paris, she now lives in London.

NATASHA LEHRER is a writer, translator, editor, and teacher. Her essays and reviews have appeared in *The Guardian*, *The Observer* (London), *The Times Literary Supplement*, *The Nation*, *Frieze*, and other journals. As literary editor of the *Jewish Quarterly* she has worked with writers including Deborah Levy, George Prochnik, and Joanna Rakoff. She has contributed to several books, most recently *Looking for an Enemy: 8 Essays on Antisemitism*. She has translated over two dozen books, including works by Georges Bataille, Robert Desnos, Amin Maalouf, Vanessa Springora, and Chantal Thomas. In 2016, she won the Scott Moncrieff Prize for *Suite for Barbara Loden* by Nathalie Léger. She lives in Paris.